What Faith Has Meant to Me

What Faith Has Meant to Me

Edited by

CLAUDE A. FRAZIER

THE WESTMINSTER PRESS
Philadelphia

BOOK DESIGN BY DOROTHY ALDEN SMITH

Published by The Westminster Press ®
Philadelphia, Pennsylvania

PRINTED IN THE UNITED STATES OF AMERICA

Library of Congress Cataloging in Publication Data

Frazier, Claude Albee, 1920–
What faith has meant to me.

1. Faith. 2. Witness bearing (Christianity)
I. Title.
BV4637.F69   234 .2   75–2054
ISBN 0–664–24825–X

1889474

On this 25th anniversary
of his work in mass evangelism
this book is dedicated
to Ruth and Billy Graham
in appreciation of
their service to God

Contents

Foreword

Say "teacher" and everyone has some mental picture. Say "doctor" and nearly all of us have had some personal experience with a family doctor. Say "pastor" and even the nonreligious have some notion of what a pastor is and does. Say "theologian" and most of us draw a blank. We have no firsthand knowledge of a "theologian." Even the word feels a bit odd and icy.

Dr. Claude Frazier's compilation of the personal thoughts and feelings of a wide range of theologians about their religion serves all of us. Note the uses of this book:

1. Theologians become very warm and human. The idea of the "superbrain" falls away in the words of these real people. They met God in ways that ordinary people can identify with. They wrestled with doubts. They tried other ways. But now in the faith of a child they stand with us.

2. Personal religion can be held by intelligent people. Too quickly too many have assumed that personal religion is for the simple; a philosophy of life is for the keen minds. Here is one of the greatest values of this book. Smart people can believe and give themselves to Christ. In fact, it is out of the personal faith that the religion of the mind evolves.

3. Faith can be systematic. Secular people tend to have sloppy theology. From a pop song, from the doubts of an attractive teacher, or a slap at the faith taken by the writer of a magazine article come many of the assumptions and ideas that comprise the man-on-the-street theology of millions of

7

people. Religious ideas, moreover, can be gathered and organized. Philosophy and religion are not the same, but there is a kinship between them. Some hard thinking would do worlds of good for our prevalent "pop theology." This book can be a sort of primer nudging us in the right direction. These writers have thought about what they believe, and they do not just believe anything and everything.

WHAT FAITH HAS MEANT TO ME will naturally attract those who already have a faith. More important, this title could mean the most to those who wander in a faith desert. Faith can mean everything to those who have none.

CECIL E. SHERMAN, Pastor
First Baptist Church
Asheville, North Carolina

Editor's Preface

WHAT DOES FAITH MEAN TO THOSE WHO HAVE SPENT MOST OF their lifetime probing life's deeper meanings and have made the study of God their occupation? What is the personal faith of theologians and notable theologians?

Today mankind stands in greater need of great affirmations than ever before in history. We are living in an age of great confusion. Persons of all ages are desperately searching for truths they can affirm. They are interested in hearing what others believe, particularly those who teach and write in the field of theology, and those who hold positions of leadership in the churches.

Recently I edited a book entitled *Notable Personalities and Their Faith.* It contained the testimonies of persons from all walks of life. I have received many favorable comments from readers of the book, and many have told me they would like to see more books of this nature. Quite a number, who were ministers, said they would like to see a book on the personal faith of theologians.

Believing that theologians would be willing to share their personal faith with others, I wrote to a considerable number, asking them to tell of their faith, their convictions, and their inner thoughts. I invited them also to relate personal incidents and experiences in which faith had a bearing on their lives.

The response was wholly gratifying. Many more testimonials were received than could be included in this book. I was deeply moved and my personal faith was strengthened as I read the stimulating and candid contributions from a wide variety of faith orientations and points of view. A former professor of a theological seminary graciously translated for me the article by Helmut Thielicke. I found his comment interesting: "All my life I have been an admirer of Thielicke, and it is now hard for me to believe that I have the opportunity to translate his great contribution from German into English for Dr. Frazier's book."

WHAT FAITH HAS MEANT TO ME is not a collection of sermons. Neither is it a gathering of theological essays. It is what I hoped it would be, a series of testimonies written in the first person by men and women telling of their own experiences in coming to faith, and what faith has meant to them in their personal lives.

I would like to extend my sincere appreciation to the contributors to this book, and to Dr. Jim Blevins for translating the Thielicke essay from German to English.

                                                    C.A.F.

G. R. Beasley-Murray

GEORGE RAYMOND BEASLEY-MURRAY WAS BORN IN London in 1916. He received his B.D. from Spurgeon's College, London; Th.M. from King's College, University of London; and Ph.D. from the same institution. He also holds a B.A. and an M.A. from Jesus College, University of Cambridge; and he received a D.D. from the University of London in 1963.

He was pastor of the Ashurst Drive Baptist Church, Ilford, Essex, from 1941 to 1948, and was pastor of Zion Chapel, Cambridge, from 1948 to 1950. For the next six years he was lecturer in New Testament Language and Literature at Spurgeon's College. He then became New Testament professor at the Baptist Theological Seminary in Ruschlikon, Zurich. He was called from this position to be principal of Spurgeon's College, a post he held from 1958 until 1973. Currently he is Visiting Professor of New Testament Interpretation at the Southern Baptist Theological Seminary in Louisville, Kentucky.

His writings include *Christ Is Alive, Jesus and the Future, Preaching the Gospel from the Gospels, A Commentary on Mark Thirteen, Baptism in the New Testament,* and *The Resurrection of Jesus Christ.* He has also contributed to *The New Bible Commentary,* the new *Peake's Commentary on the Bible,* and The Broadman Bible Commentary. He was also a translator and the general editor of Rudolf Bultmann's classic commentary on the Gospel of John.

11

The Clue
to the Meaning of Life

G. R. BEASLEY-MURRAY

GOD BECAME THE ACKNOWLEDGED CENTER OF MY LIFE WHEN first I grasped that in Jesus Christ the holy and almighty love of God was at work for the life of the world, and therefore for my sake.

God continues to be the center of my life because I am held captive by that same almighty love revealed in Jesus.

For me faith from start to finish is bound up with the significance of Jesus Christ, the Lord.

The story of a man's faith can never be fully told, for we are all the product of countless influences, known and unknown, from birth and even before. I passed through my childhood practically unscathed by religious influences, apart from a few vivid memories of services that I attended in a Roman Catholic church in my very early years. My introduction to Christianity as a power to be reckoned with began just prior to my fifteenth birthday. A boy of my own age moved from the north of England to the city in which I lived, and we came to know each other. He was a football enthusiast, and he speedily discovered that a football club was attached to a church in our neighborhood. The condition for belonging to the club was attendance at the men's Bible class. My friend was willing to pay this price to play football, but he did not wish to go to the class alone, so he urged me to accompany him. My protestations were in vain; religious or irreligious scruples were of no account when a game of soccer was at stake! So off to the Bible class we went. It proved to be a more attractive affair than I had imagined.

The members of the class were, in fact, men, not youths, but they were all very friendly—and the leader was a saint of a man. His endeavors to expound the Bible were not very successful. He wrote out his addresses with painstaking care, and steadfastly kept his eyes directed to his manuscript as he read every word of it, while the members of the class chattered to one another or otherwise diverted themselves! Nevertheless his was a gracious and lovable personality, with a kindness and a goodness that made a deep impression upon me. On reflection, I think that my first conscious steps to God were taken because of the embodiment of Christian character in that man.

Two weeks after my initial visit to the Bible class my friend moved to another section of our city. I have never seen him since; I cannot even recall his name. But my feet had been set on a new path, with momentous consequences. It is difficult for me not to trace the hand of God at work through this strange encounter.

From the Bible class I was graduated to the church services, to learn more of the faith to which I had been introduced, and which was becoming of increasing interest to me. I found a wider circle of people to whom God mattered more than anything else, and their mode of talking about him and even talking to him impressed me. Then came a mission in the church, led by two students who were preparing for the Christian ministry at Spurgeon's College. They were maturer men than the average theological student, I later realized, and had had a wider experience of life than many of their contemporaries. Their preaching of the good news brought to a head a process that was rapidly accelerating in my mind. One night the sermon was devoted to the meaning of Christ's giving of himself upon the cross. For the first time in my life it became clear to me that when Christ died for the world in its sin he included me in the scope of his sacrifice. It was an overwhelming discovery. "The Son of God . . . loved me and gave himself for me": the conviction that Paul had voiced seized my heart, and the love of God in Christ called out from me an answering repentance and faith and love. On that day I began life afresh under the authority of Christ the Lord in dependence on him as Redeemer for every step of my way.

Since that trembling step of faith was taken at the immature age of fifteen, more than forty years have passed. How do I view it now at this distance of time? I have thought of it very often. In the intervening years I have had the opportunity of encountering a great variety of ideas about God and Christ and man in this world, from the devout to the skeptical and hostile. Having been born during World War I, I felt that the experience of World War II was ever more tragic. I have pondered the kaleidoscopic international scene in the subsequent years, have marveled at the feats of my contemporaries in their explorations of outer space. I have been equally horrified at the cold calculations of experts in nuclear war, as they reckon the effectiveness of their weapons in terms of the millions of men these weapons can destroy. I have sought to understand an age that lives as though God were dead. In particular, I have considered the ways of those I know best, Christian and non-Christian, comparing their experiences of life with mine. The upshot of it all is that I stand today where I did as a youth, in the shadow of the cross of Christ, grateful for the love that gave itself for me and for all men, and in utter dependence on the Lover.

The difference between my faith now and my faith then is chiefly that I understand better the implications of that sacrifice and what called it forth: the grim reality of sin and its destructive power in the world, the inevitability of God's resistance to it in his holiness, and the astonishing grace that moved him to deliver man from it. The cross disturbs me now, more than it did in my earlier years, for the romance that tends to surround it has been replaced by a fuller realization of its horror. Correspondingly the man who died on it draws me to himself even more powerfully. I understand more clearly the uniqueness of his action, when he stood before God for the entire race of man, rendering an obedience which was their due but which they could not give, and experiencing the desolation which they would fain escape but cannot.

It would not have occurred to me in my younger days to describe God's love as "almighty." I have now come to recognize that he who gave himself for the life of the world achieved his end by virtue of his resurrection. Historically there is little doubt that if the last glimpse the disciples had of Jesus was of the man on his cross on Good Friday, none would have heard of him today. For when Christ died, faith in him died too. It was the events of Easter Sunday that enabled his followers to perceive that the cross was not simply a terrible tragedy wrought by sin, but a means of redemption from sin. The resurrection showed that God as well as man was involved in the cross—God in Christ, reconciling the world to himself, as Paul put it (II Cor. 5:19). The conjunction of Good Friday and Easter Sunday enabled the followers of Jesus to grasp that in that twin event the turn of the ages took place. The promised era of salvation, otherwise known as the kingdom of God, had arrived, and in fellowship with the risen Lord men could experience its powers. With it came forgiveness of sins, the knowledge of God, the presence of the Holy Spirit, release from bondage, and fear for a life of true freedom and rejoicing in the peace of God. A transformed relationship with God and with all his children gave a purpose for life culminating in being agents in God's reconciliation of all men through Christ. All this and more is the issue of the death and resurrection of Christ. In that deed almighty love in truth is revealed, for from his death has come life for the world. In the last resort it is none other than the divine life that Christ gives, for the Spirit he sends binds us to him, and in and through him we are linked with the source of life which death cannot quench.

In a word, God's gift to man through Christ is *life*. More specifically, it is life under God's gracious rule, wherein the things that spoil and ruin our earthly existence have no place and the purpose of God in creating us comes to fruition. Under this present mode of existence it has admittedly only begun; but it has really and decisively begun. If that life needs the environment of a superior mode of existence to bring it to perfection, the essential condition needed to bring it to pass

has already come about. For this reason the moment of ultimate concern to a Christian is neither his birth nor his death,
but his transition from life out of Christ to life in Christ. He
who is one with Christ has shared in the most important death
that has ever taken place, i.e., the death on the cross. Similarly
he has shared in the resurrection on the third day, which
cannot be undone; he is thus reborn into the eternal kingdom.
If that sounds like riddles to some ears, it is the heart of what
Paul believed and of what John learned; it sums up the meaning of life to me. It is worth making the effort to grasp it. See
John 3:1–16; 5:24; 10:10; Rom. 6:1–11; II Cor. 5:14–21; Gal.
2:20.

John and Paul are perhaps the supreme interpreters of Jesus,
but they would ask us to listen to Jesus for ourselves and not
simply to them. This very thing I gladly seek to do. I count it
as one of the blessings of my life that for some years part of
my responsibility as a teacher has been to join with my students
in studying the life and teaching of Jesus as they are recorded
in the Gospels. I deliberately put it that way, rather than
convey the impression that I know *all* about Jesus. It is part
of the greatness of Jesus that he constantly eludes our grasp.
His vocabulary is simple, his mode of speech for the most part
is direct, and the pictures by which he illuminates his teaching
are all drawn from the world of his hearers. We do right
therefore to encourage children to read the Gospels and to
instruct them in their meaning. Unreflective men and women
can similarly read the Gospels to their profit, and be inspired
by the wisdom and the stories recounted therein. It remains
true, however, that there are profundities in the Gospels that
challenge the finest minds to plumb their depths. Jesus himself
is recorded as saying, "All things have been delivered to me by
my Father; and no one knows the Son except the Father, and
no one knows the Father except the Son and any one to whom
the Son chooses to reveal him" (Matt. 11:27). In virtue of such
a unique relation to God and knowledge of God he calls on
men: "Come to me, all who labor and are heavy laden, and I
will give you rest. Take my yoke upon you, and learn from me;

for I am gentle and lowly in heart, and you will find rest for your souls" (Matt. 11:28–29). Such words are addressed to the intelligent and the moral as well as to the fools and the immoral, and they proceed from a consciousness which Jesus possessed of standing in a unique relation to the Father. This claim of Jesus I accept, and I see no hope of a rival anywhere. In him I see the ultimate authority of God and the meaning of life in this world. In him I see the one through whom God's saving sovereignty entered into the world, so that to be in touch with him was and is to be in touch with the saving power of God. He is one of us and one with all men, so that he stood and stands as representative for all men. Yet on his own confession he was and is one with the Father, the representative not alone of men in their need but of God in his power to deliver, whose kingdom shall know no end.

There are passages in the Gospels that tell of the climax of God's dealings with his world, and in them Jesus, the Son of God, has a central part to play, even as he had in his death and resurrection for mankind. We speak of that event as the Second Coming of Christ. The language used to describe the events of that time is symbolic, and is characteristic of him who loved to speak in pictures and parables. The last book of the Bible, which deals especially with this theme, is full of pictures of the end. At times they seem more like the cartoons of a Picasso than the portraits of a Rubens. From all these representations, however, one thing stands clear: he who was God's instrument for the initiation of the world's salvation is the one who will complete it. He who brought into being the new world of life from death will bring it to its climax in the triumph of life over death in the world (or rather, as the book of Revelation teaches, in the universe itself). He who performs that work of God shares the nature of God. The end will reveal to all what he has been from the beginning. Any man who understands that now will not hesitate to acknowledge Jesus the Christ as Thomas did, when he faced the risen Christ in the wake of the first Easter: "My Lord and my God!" (John 20:28).

It will be evident that the foregoing was not intended to describe a system of theology, or a formal creed such as would be recited in church. Rather, it is offered as a confession of faith that sees in Jesus the clue to God and to the meaning of life. This faith is the inspiration of my life. I gladly own my unity with all who share it. I ask of no man that he use my language in trying to spell it out, for the Lord Christ is greater than all our efforts to explain him. But I am encouraged that the people of God are more able to speak with a united voice about Jesus as the Revealer and Redeemer than they are in their attempts to describe the nature of the church and its worship and organization. I would be disturbed if the reverse were true. As it is, I gladly declare my indebtedness to the churches with whom I am in closest fellowship and whom I serve (the Baptist). I also acknowledge my equal indebtedness to a multitude of Christians of all the major denominations who have enriched my life in the process of common study, worship, and service, and not least by their friendship. I have nothing that has not been given to me, and I am conscious of having received everything of worth in the fellowship of Christ's church.

My appreciation of the value of worship has deepened with the passing of the years. Despite the failures which from time to time have marked the churches' efforts to minister to the world, I believe that the church, and the church alone, can bring that life to the world which God ever waits to bestow.

To serve God and man in the fellowship of the church is the greatest privilege a man can receive. Therein he may discover himself, and God, and the meaning of existence. And in the discovery he finds life.

William Hugh Brownlee

WILLIAM HUGH BROWNLEE GREW UP ON A KANSAS farm. He attended Sterling College and Pittsburgh-Xenia Theological Seminary, earning the degrees of Th.B. and Th.M. His graduate study was at Duke University, where he earned his Ph.D. He studied also at the American School of Oriental Research in Jerusalem in 1947–1948, being one of the first scholars to work on the Dead Sea Scrolls.

Among the major awards that he has received are the Jamieson Scholarship from Pittsburgh-Xenia, the Gurney Harris Kearns Fellowship from Duke, appointment as Fellow of the American Schools of Oriental Research, Fellow of the American Association of Theological Schools, Fellow of the American Council of Learned Societies, and Fellow of the American Philosophical Society. He is also a member of Phi Beta Kappa, and holds a D.D. from Sterling College.

He was pastor of a United Presbyterian congregation in Newton, Kansas, he has taught at Duke University, and since 1959 has been professor of religion at Claremont Graduate School, Claremont, California. His writings, primarily on Old Testament subjects and the Dead Sea Scrolls, are too numerous to list. His major work was *The Meaning of the Qumrân Scrolls for the Bible: With Special Attention to the Book of Isaiah.* He also wrote the commentary on Ezekiel in *The Interpreter's One-Volume Commentary on the Bible.*

Faith
and Criticism Are Allies

WILLIAM HUGH BROWNLEE

HOW DOES A KANSAS FARM BOY OF SIMPLE FAITH IN GOD PASS
through the various levels of higher education and still retain
his faith? The answer to that question is the story of my life,
which with all its formative influences is too long to be recounted here.

God's grace reached me in my early childhood, making of
me an avid reader of the Bible, which I read through and
pondered through many times. By the time I reached high
school age, I knew that God wanted me to study for the
ministry. Knowing Jesus Christ was always a source of joy and
song. When working alone in the field, I spent most of the day
singing. Sometimes I sang familiar psalms and hymns; but
more often I was composing impromptu my own songs of
praise. When others were around, I kept the melodies in my
heart; but all day, no matter if I worked as much as fourteen
hours, was filled with joy. The Lord had become my strength
and my song.

In Sterling College I met other committed Christian young
people and found in their friendship a source of increased joy.
I bore my personal witness to Christ in many ways and par-
ticipated in many church services of the Gospel Team. With
my eyes clearly focused on the Christian ministry, I studied
broadly, but majored in English literature. I learned Greek as
an essential tool for interpreting the New Testament.

In the fall of 1939 I enrolled at Pittsburgh-Xenia Theological Seminary, a small, scholarly, evangelical school. Three

years' study greatly expanded my acquaintance with the Christian heritage in a wide spectrum of fields that we were all required to study. Here I added Hebrew to Greek as a further aid to understanding the Bible. In courses dealing with church history, philosophy of religion, systematic theology, and Biblical archaeology I learned that the Christian message can be both elucidated and rationally defended. The professors were not only learned but they were dedicated Christians who imparted to others the desire to preach with vigor and with joy the good news of Jesus Christ. If the purpose of the Scriptures is to equip the man of God for the ministry, we were well equipped; for we had studied most of the Bible while in seminary, much of it in the original language.

The seminary had a tradition of awarding annually a scholarship to one senior to enable him to study for a year at the University of Edinburgh, during which he would write a thesis for the Master of Theology degree to be submitted to the home seminary. Thus when I completed my Bachelor of Theology degree in Pittsburgh, I was awarded the Jamieson Scholarship for this extra year of study. Actually one of my classmates had a grade point average, a small fraction of 1 percent higher than mine, but he preferred to pass up this opportunity. Actually, even I was not prepared to use it immediately. The United States entered World War II during our last year in seminary and many ministers had volunteered for the chaplaincy. This meant a shortage of ministers in the churches. To spend an extra year in study at that time seemed like disloyalty both to the church and to our country. Still I hoped to use this scholarship, delaying use of it until after the war.

One could not then get a passport to study abroad, so I wanted to wait until the war was over to do my stint of study. The decision rested with the Board of Education of the United Presbyterian Church, of which the president of the seminary was an influential member. He encouraged me to believe that this was possible, so I took a temporary pastorate at Newton, Kansas. At the end of my first year there, I was urged by the Board of Education to use my scholarship at once in some

American university, but I informed them that I had volunteered for the chaplaincy in the Navy and would need to await the outcome of the application. My eyesight did not measure up to the requirements, but the authorities in Kansas City told me that sometimes exceptions were granted, and so I hoped that mine would be such a case. I never did hear officially from my application until I telephoned the headquarters in Kansas City the next spring, when once more the Board of Education were demanding that I quit the pastorate and return to school. By this time they were so indignant with me that they wrote somewhat as follows: "You go back to school starting this summer, or you will forfeit the scholarship."

I loved the people of my congregation. I had invested nearly two full years of hard work in preaching and pastoral care, but I accepted it as God's will that I go on to graduate school. An examination of graduate school programs made me most interested in Johns Hopkins or Yale University, but neither institution offered any courses for graduate credit in religion during the summer of 1944. Only Duke University had a live program of summer offerings, so I decided to enter there, with the idea that if I were not satisfied, I could transfer to another university in the autumn. One of the prime attractions at Johns Hopkins was the presence on the faculty of William F. Albright; but his brother-in-law, William F. Stinespring, at Duke University, was a rival attraction. I had heard of him as a friend of Professor James L. Kelso, of Pittsburgh-Xenia. All three men had shared archaeological experiences in Palestine.

Duke University presented me with a new theological and intellectual climate. Some of the faculty members of the Divinity School, as in most liberal theological seminaries (both then and now), were hostile to evangelical Christianity. Being ignorant of the intellectual and spiritual depth of evangelical scholarship, they caricatured evangelical positions. Beginning seminary students from conservative backgrounds were often confused and shaken in their faith; and when they emerged from the first shock they too often had little doctrinal substance left with which to nourish their faith throughout their ministerial careers. I encountered this hostile atmosphere not only in my contacts with certain professors but also among some students with whom I studied, ate, and lived. By the end of my first summer, I was tempted to turn away in disgust from the realm of higher critical scholarship to a noncritical conservatism which assumes the inerrancy of every word of the inspired authors, but leaves room for determining more accurately what those inspired words were through textual criticism of the Bible in the original tongues. Those who pursue such a course are at least rooted in the great doctrines of the church through the ages, and their primary concern is not sophistry, but to understand the gospel and to live by it.

After my solid grounding at Pittsburgh-Xenia Theological Seminary, I was not easily misled by caricatures of evangelical faith. In fact, I irritated some of my professors by challenging their distorted presentations. At the same time, by persisting in my studies, I was learning to appreciate the problems raised by literary and historical criticism. In fact, in the fall of 1944 I began an independent study of the critical problems connected with The Book of Ezekiel. The study of this book would open up many serious questions. The reason for my choice of this book was not only its fascinating character but also that it was one book of the Old Testament to which little attention was given in my seminary training. I was determined to understand the whole Bible. One of my professors at Pittsburgh-Xenia had confessed frankly that there were many problems connected with this book of whose solution he was uncertain, but he had indicated only briefly what these problems were. Old Testament introductions, of course, brought out the critical issues. Yet, in order to guarantee complete objectivity in my research, I decided not to read any critical commentary until I had read the entire text of Ezekiel in Hebrew, for I wanted first of all to study the text firsthand without any passage-by-passage guidance or misguidance, whichever the case might be. After I completed this task, I would turn to a study of critical works dealing with Ezekiel; and I hoped to be able to prove that Ezekiel's prophetic ministry was in Babylonia and not in

Palestine, and that it was the critics of Ezekiel (and not the prophet!) who were mentally unbalanced!

My general impression of The Book of Ezekiel from reading the Hebrew alone was twofold: (1) a general unity and (2) considerable textual corruption. As I pursued my reading, I was persuaded by the evidence that Ezekiel was a Palestinian, rather than an Exilic prophet. Similarly, in my exegetical studies with Professor Judah Goldin, I became convinced that Deuteronomy was a reinterpretation of earlier Pentateuchal sources and that it was most probably written during the reign of Manasseh. It could not, therefore, contain literal speeches by Moses. It was rather the application of Mosaic traditions to conditions of the seventh century B.C. Ascription of the book, in its present form, to Moses was a sort of Semitic idiom to be illustrated in other literary areas. Thus there was a tendency to ascribe all wisdom literature to Solomon, including the Book of Wisdom written in the first century B.C. In the case of the Torah, the completion of the Pentateuch did not conclude the process, but the Oral Law continued until the writing of the Mishnah and the compiling of the Talmud with its numerous and massive tomes; and this Oral Law in all its ramifications was traced back to Moses! This meant that the Scriptures were not verbally infallible from a rigidly literalistic point of view.

These critical discoveries, together with the antievangelical attitude of many with whom I lived, made me fearful for a time whether my own faith could stand the strain. If not every detail in the Bible was true, could one rely upon anything in it? Already in my seminary doctrinal thesis, I had indicated hypothetically that, despite my then adherence to the doctrine of plenary inspiration, if anything could ever establish any historical inaccuracy in the Bible, it would still be possible to hold to the moral and spiritual infallibility of the Scriptures. In the case of Deuteronomy, however, as I now could see, one constantly witnessed a revision of older laws in order to make them more humane. If such revisions were needed and were not merely reapplications to new circumstances, then much of the earliest material was not morally infallible. Thus there was a double-

pronged challenge to my faith in the verbal inerrancy of the
Scriptures.

To meet this challenge, I turned to God in prayer. For
privacy I took long walks, deep into the woods that surrounded
the campus at Duke. There I read the Bible devotionally,
prayed, and sang hymns and Biblical psalms aloud. I knew from
many years of experience that God was real; but what I needed
was his constant companionship and the illumination he could
bring to my present perplexities. As I let my faith soar through
song and prayer, there came an ever deeper assurance that my
life was in the hand of Christ and that around the hand of
Christ was the hand of the Father, so that nothing in historical
criticism or in liberal disparagements of the gospel could ever
wrest me from the loving hand of God. If Christ is the Truth,
then I need not fear the truth, for if I followed it far enough,
it would always lead to Christ and through him to the full
knowledge of God. The Bible is also like that. Follow out every
facet of morality or theological understanding, pursuing it to
the very end of the Bible. What this leads to is that teaching
which is perfect, reviving the soul, and that commandment
which is pure and righteous altogether, bringing joy and moral
enlightenment to the heart. The reliability of the Bible for
faith and life is to be found in the Bible as a whole, not in every
portion of it in separation from the total message. Still one
must not suppose a gradual evolution, a sort of inclined plane
leading up to the heights of the New Testament. There is
much of unsurpassable moral and spiritual grandeur in early as
well as in later material; and there may be some portions of the
New Testament that do not reach the heights of others. Yet
the Christ is there in the Scriptures, and infallibly so for those
who seek. He is the true and living way to the Father. This
assurance was the answer to my prayers. I have never forgotten
what I learned in the woods at Duke. It is this which has given
meaning and relevance to all my study and research.

Another answer to my prayers grew out of my initial insist-
ence upon reading the entire Book of Ezekiel in Hebrew before
reading the critical commentaries. When during the summer

of 1945 I noticed how certain commentaries questioned the authenticity of chapter 34, because verse 6 portrayed the Jews as "scattered over all the face of the earth," I picked up my Hebrew Bible to look at the text more carefully. There I discovered in my Hebrew Bible the penciled comment, "high places." At once the reminiscence of what must have run through my mind when first writing that was recalled. Having seen some of the language of this verse used in connection with the illicit hilltop shrines of the Old Testament, I considered translating the verse: "My flock are gone astray on all hills and upon every lofty height! My flock are scattered all over the face of the land; no one seeks, no one searches for them." As I read on, I must have noticed that after verse 11, there is a hopeful promise of a regathering of the nation from many lands. Since this is antithetical to the earlier verses, verse 6 must have been meant as rendered in the American Standard Version that the sheep were scattered all over the *earth*, and the reference to the mountains and the hills was only poetic metaphor for this dispersal. If I had been following a commentary, this would have been evident from the first, and the other interpretation would have never occurred to me. The amazing thing is that I had allowed my initial comment to stand, there to be reconsidered at a later time. Thus the present upshot was the exciting idea that perhaps 34:1–10 did originally indict the rulers of the nation (the shepherds of the flock) of self-serving and of neglecting the flock by allowing them to worship (go astray) at the forbidden hilltop shrines and not just at Jerusalem. Then at a later date this was reapplied as poetic metaphor for the dispersion of the Jews. This would mean that in verses 1–10 we had an original oracle of doom by the prophet and that in the rest of the chapter we have supplemental material from a later time. Through further study I discovered that the original oracle consisted of a whole series of tristich, poetic lines, into which brief prose commentary had been inserted. I was then prepared to make some important contributions to the literary criticism of The Book of Ezekiel.

The result of my researches on Ezekiel was an interest to

prepare more than a master's thesis, which I did in a Th.M. thesis submitted to Pittsburgh-Xenia early in 1946. I continued my work for a Ph.D. at Duke University, which I completed in 1947.

At the same time I received a fellowship from the American Schools of Oriental Research for study in Jerusalem in 1947–1948. Providentially this opened up for me the opportunity to share in the first discoveries of the Dead Sea Scrolls and to translate the first scrolls, the ancient Habakkuk Commentary and the Manual of Discipline. Responsibilities for interpreting these ancient manuscripts have delayed my publication of extensive materials regarding the prophet Ezekiel; and yet in *The Interpreter's One-Volume Commentary on the Bible* I have contributed material that marks important progress beyond my earliest work, which in many respects was marked by immaturity. When *The Jerusalem Bible* appeared with its marginal comment to Ezek. 34:6, "Probably alluding to worship on the 'high places,' " I was thrilled, for an early article by me had succeeded in transferring my penciled comment into the margin of an important new version of the Bible. Now also the *New English Bible* reflects my understanding in its translation of the same verse.

Faith and open-minded, critical research have worked hand in hand in seeking out the real meanings of the Bible. God has blessed my labors when pursued through faith. My prayer to God is that he will continue to bless my work whether in interpreting the Bible or other relevant literature as a means of deepening and enriching the understanding and the faith of all God's people. Criticism and faith are not enemies but allies, as one searches the Scriptures daily.

David Cairns

DAVID CAIRNS WAS BORN IN AYTON, BERWICKSHIRE,
Scotland, in 1904. He has served as a minister in the
Church of Scotland since his ordination in 1935. He
has an M.A. degree from Oxford University, and a
D.D. from the University of Edinburgh.

For five years he was pastor of a congregation of the
Church of Scotland in Bridge of Allen, and during
World War II was chaplain to a Scottish division that
saw action in France, Belgium, Holland, and Germany. Following this experience, he became professor
of practical theology at Christ's College, Aberdeen,
and reader in systematic theology at Aberdeen University, a position he held until his retirement in 1972.
For ten years he was a member of the Faith and Order
Commission of the World Council of Churches.

Among his numerous published works, *The Image
of God in Man* was reissued in an enlarged paperback
edition after twenty-two years. Other titles include *A
Gospel Without Myth?, Rudolf Bultmann's Challenge to the Preacher, God Up There? A Study in
Divine Transcendence,* and *In Remembrance of Me,
Aspects of the Lord's Supper.* He has also translated
a number of books into English, notably the third
volume of Emil Brunner's *Dogmatics.*

Why I Believe

SOME YEARS AGO A SERIES OF TALKS ON THE BRITISH RADIO were published under the title *Why I Believe.* On reading them, I noted that a number of the contributors dealt with the theme in a very impersonal manner. What has been explicitly asked of the contributors to this present book is something much more personal, and I shall try to comply, though I am aware of the dangers of appearing self-satisfied and self-centered.

No doubt one of the main causes of my faith has been the Christian inheritance into which I was born, and in which I have been fortunate to live all my life. I hope to show that this inheritance has not just been a main cause of my belief, but a real reason for it.

I was born into a Christian family, into the tradition of Scottish Presbyterianism, and yet through experience of the world of thought and through contact with Christian people of many denominations and nationalities, the circle in which I grew up had deep sympathies with many other traditions. On my father's side there was a long line of ministers and humble people in the Scottish Borders, notably shepherds and farm workers. On my mother's side there was a rather more prosperous line of well-doing and godly farmers.

Since my mother died when I was a child, the main spiritual influence in my youth was undoubtedly that of my father. He was deeply involved in the work of the Edinburgh Missionary Conference in 1910, and in the work of the Student Christian

Movement in its most hopeful and expansive days. This brought into our family circle many religious leaders and pioneers both from Europe and from America. My father and his family were prolific letter writers, and of late I have been going through family correspondence. Looking back through the letters of three generations, I have received a very strong impression of the integrity, beauty, and attractiveness of the lives these letters reveal. Thus my first impression of Christianity was one that required very little correction. Through these letters and the memories that they recall, there shone an affection which did not lack in humor and breadth of intellectual sympathy. As I think of them, the phrase "a cloud of witnesses" comes forcibly to mind. Though these people are now dead, I feel that I belong together with them, and always shall, and I am conscious of their support and continuing affection. I do not idolize them—they had their failings and limitations —but a man cannot come into such an inheritance and recognize it for what it is without a deep sense of gratitude for it.

Another preliminary note must be made. From childhood I have had a strong sense of wonder and of the sacred, which made me early appreciate the thought of William Wordsworth, a sense of atmosphere and communion with nature that has always been a joy to me. The silence of the mountains after sunset and music like Beethoven's *The Archduke Trio* have always spoken to me poignantly of God. Though the vividness of early experiences has to some extent faded, they have left something with me that I hope I shall never lose. As Wordsworth has expressed it:

> the soul,
> Remembering how she felt, but what she felt
> Remembering not, retains an obscure sense
> Of possible sublimity.

These early experiences have perhaps made it easier for me to believe. Though the mystery, for example, of effective intercession is no more explicable to me than to others, I do not find a great difficulty in believing it.

Looking back on nearly seventy years of experience, I am continually reminded of what an extraordinarily rich and wonderful thing our human life can be. There is an infinity of human interests, achievements, and problems, yet there is only one question of ultimate importance. Some men seem not to be aware of it, while others confront it in different ways according to their temperament and the climate of the age. Sometimes the question comes to the individual in his loneliness and despair: "What must I do to be saved?"—though he may not often, in these days, put it in just these terms. Sometimes it comes to us when we are faced by death or misfortune to someone we love: "What is the meaning of things?" For reflective people it may come in more general terms: "What is the meaning of history, of this human life of ours, with its vast cosmic back-curtain of the stars, man's long inheritance, our own life, coming from mystery and soon going out into mystery?"

It seems to me that all literature, all serious historical writing, all art, even all music, is a comment or interpretation or inspiration somehow connected with this great question.

And in the end, as I see it, it comes to this: "Are we alone in the world, the best efforts of a great blind struggling force, or is there help for humanity?" Has a great and decisive word been spoken from beyond which changes everything, which gives humanity a hope and a goal? This has been the main problem that I have been fortunate to have had time to ponder, from the days of my youth, when my father and I discussed it, when I studied theology in Germany and Switzerland and brought back from there challenges and questions. It is the problem to which I have given twenty-five years of my life, teaching divinity students and preparing them for the ministry.

Sometimes at night, when we waken from sleep, we see everything with a preternatural clarity. Often the supposed illumination dissipates into sheer nonsense when seen in the sober light of morning, but not always. And I regard the experience that I shall set down here as one of the central ones of my life.

As a student, between the wars, I was coming back from Oberammergau with friends, where we had attended the Passion Play. We were traveling by train at night, sitting in a compartment full of passengers, traveling down the banks of the Rhine. I awakened suddenly, to see the name of a station dimly illuminated, as I remember, by a lamp. It was Rheinbrühl, and this name awakened in me a host of memories. As a student at Oxford I had studied ancient history, and I recalled that Rheinbrühl had marked the boundary between the provinces of the Upper Rhine and the Lower Rhine in the days of the early Roman Empire. This brought back to my mind the strange fierce story of the first century A.D. as related by Tacitus in his *Histories,* a tale of marches and countermarches, sieges and battles, with the trackless forests to the west continually threatening the Roman soldiers and citizens of the garrison towns. They had long since disappeared, these men and women, with their loves and hopes, sins, anxieties, and all their eager activities. Outside, the great river was flowing swiftly and silently down through Germany and Holland, out to the sea, to be lost there. Was the river of history like this, flowing turbulently or silently—nowhere?

The train began to move again, slowly at first and then faster. Electric standards stood beside the line, and as we passed them, their cold light flashed for a moment on the faces of the sleeping passengers and then left them in darkness. I could see now how they had looked as children, how they would look when they were old, how they would look when they were dead. Then suddenly into my inner ear there came the words, not in a ghostly way, but vibrant in the tones of the voice of Alois Lang, the Oberammergau Christ, which I had so recently heard, "I am the resurrection and the life: he that believeth in me, though he were dead, yet shall he live. And whosoever liveth and believeth in me shall never die." And then I was sure of hope, both for men and for the river of history, that it would not disappear into an ocean of meaninglessness, but would reach its fulfillment.

This has been the faith that has grown upon me from my

youth. I have had times of depression. One such time I was
encouraged by a fellow chaplain in the Army, who told me that
he was sure I had a good deal more faith than I knew. This
turned out to be a real word of God to me. And, strangely,
when in action in the war, though never under the stress or
danger that came to others, I found, and confirmed with my
fellow chaplains, that our faith burned not dimmer but
brighter.

I have since then been faced with situations from which
there was no way out but forward, and if the way forward had
not opened out, then all would have been up. But the way did
open out. I felt assured that, God willing, I would live perma-
nently in more assurance than before this experience.

As I go on in life, I become convinced more and more that
we do not deal with a situation in which we are forced to cope
entirely unaided, but we are the children of a God whose
pleasure it is always to surprise us by his power and generosity.

Further, I am realizing more and more that our whole life
is a dialogue with our Creator, and that the people who surround us—wife, children, friends, and colleagues—are the gifts
to us of an immeasurable kindness for which we must be
grateful.

If I were asked what for me is the simple center of the
Christian faith, I would quote Rom. 8:14–17: "The Spirit you
have received is not a spirit of slavery, leading you back into
a life of fear, but a Spirit that makes us sons, enabling us to cry,
'Abba, Father.' In that cry the Spirit of God joins with our
spirit in testifying that we are God's children; and if children,
then heirs. We are God's heirs, and Christ's fellow-heirs, if we
share his sufferings now in order to share his splendour here-
after." (NEB)

I am aware that what I have written may appear, and may
be, rather smug and self-satisfied if the balance is not corrected.
So I hasten to add that I know—and my friends know even
better—how far short I fall in sensitivity and love, and how
poor my record has been, and how often I have to say to myself,
"If at your age you can still make blunders in personal relations

like that, what hope is there for you in your own resources?" But then I am reminded that my hope does not reside in me. Indeed, for me, Christianity has largely been a power of encouragement for one whose courage and assurance are always needing reinforcement. This is a confession of weakness, and yet, when it corresponds to the fact, one must say, "That is what I am." I seldom feel able or assured to face my problems in my own strength, but experience has taught me that in spite of this, I will get through, and each time it happens I become more convinced that help is being given.

My natural tendency is to have a continual sense of guilt. Sometimes this is attached to some difficulty or sin or failure, but more often it is vague and unattached. In any case, Christian faith gives the immense reassurance that, however we may feel, we are in fact right with God, and can at every moment start afresh in touch with him, and face the open road to which he has called us.

Having suffered for over ten years from severe osteoarthritis of the hips, and for that time having gone about on elbow crutches, four years ago by one of the miracles of modern surgery I was given a new hip joint and an absolutely unhoped-for liberation of movement and range of activities. This great blessing, I feel sure, is a sign, not only of God's goodness to me in this life but a promise that it will continue in a life that he has promised to us on the other side.

In writing about my faith, I realize that my answer has necessarily been rather introspective. I feel that something must be said to deal with the fortunes of the world. In spite of various adverse experiences, I am aware of the unusually fortunate and in some ways sheltered character of my own life. I am also very much aware of the immense amount of evil, suffering, and darkness in the world today. This is not the place to discuss the problem that evil and sin poses for believers. But it seems to me, looking out on the world around us, that there is both a great deal to be grateful for and much that is evil and threatening. The dangers and evils that confront our world call for our utmost efforts to surmount them, and humanly speaking, they may well overwhelm us. But here also, as in our individual lives, we are not alone. In this day when so many are tempted to become cynical or frightened, the task of Christians is twofold, to proclaim God's judgment, but also his mercy, and mercy predominates over judgment. We must keep calm and hopeful, sure that he is in final control and that he will not abandon the world to which he has so deeply committed himself in Christ.

Yves Congar

YVES CONGAR WAS BORN IN SEDAN, FRANCE, IN 1904. He studied in the Seminary of the Catholic Institute of Paris, and was ordained as a preaching friar in the Order of Saint Dominic. He has an M.A. degree in philosophy and a Th.D. from the Sorbonne.

He was professor of theology in the Dominican school at Saulchoir from 1931 to 1954. He is a member of the Vatican's International Commission on Theology, and holds honorary degrees from the Universities of Freibourg, Switzerland; Tübingen, Germany; Santiago, Chile; Notre Dame and the Catholic University of America in the United States.

His published writings consist of more than fifteen hundred titles of which more than thirty are books. A number of his books have been translated into English and the following are still in print: *Ecumenism and the Future of the Church, Lay People in the Church, After 900 Years,* and *History of Theology.*

Nourished by Knowledge

YVES CONGAR

THE FAITH OF MY CHILDHOOD BECAME PERSONALIZED BY MY contact with life. I was ten years old in 1914 when the World War I plunged my little country, on the borders of the Belgian frontier, into the drama of two battles and an occupation that was to last more than fifty months. An intense patriotic tension, a perpetual mild resistance to the invader (I went before the German military judge at the age of thirteen), a very hard life materially, the sight of the still greater misery of so many prisoners of all nationalities who were dying from exhaustion, the concentration of the mind on religious practice as the only area of greatness and of liberty left to us—all that prepared my soul to take seriously prayer, striving for God, the will of an active life for him.

It was in this moral climate that a priestly vocation began to assert itself in me. As a child I wanted to be a doctor. I had asked for a small microscope as a First Communion gift. At the beginning of 1918, I felt great emptiness within myself, all the more painful because I could not confide in anyone. It was in this void that the vocation to preach God to men became a call heard within me. I have never been able to doubt the reality of this interior fact. From that time my faith became identified with this vocation. The two certainties intermingled. I lived them both simultaneously.

During my military service I decided for the religious life and more precisely for that of friar preacher in the Order of Saint Dominic. After that at the Seminary of the Catholic

Institute of Paris (1921–1924), in the novitiate and the scholasticate I proved the truth of this word of Saint Augustine, who speaks of theological science as "that knowledge by which a very salutary faith is engendered in us, nourished, defended, strengthened." Yes, the study of the faith is a powerful nourishment for it. How many times have I not repeated, in congresses or meetings, the key word that Lenin gave at the first meeting of the Komsomol: "Let us learn! Learn! Learn!"

Not that I have never met with difficulty. I can even say that, very often, the question came to my mind: What if all that were just an enormous illusion, a construction of the mind, nursed for centuries by the organization called Church? What saved me personally, at least on the intellectual level, was an understanding and a knowledge of history, and also, I think, the basis of philosophical realism that I owe to Saint Thomas and the teachers who have initiated me to his thought. Mere knowledge is not sufficient to answer every doubt. It suffices all the less because there are always zones of vagueness and objections that are left not satisfied. Moreover, faith is not mere knowledge. It is first of all and fundamentally a certain disposition of the heart, an openness, an experience of the coherence of Christianity on the level of the universal direction it gives to life. That is why faith demands that it be practiced and lived. Without that, you can discuss indefinitely—you never make up your mind. To be a disciple, according to the gospel, is not only to listen to Jesus, it is to follow him. It is to feed on him, and even to "eat" him in the Eucharist; but then, it is not we who assimilate that food, rather it assimilates us unto itself! I repeat, however, that the understanding and the knowledge of history have been a very positive help to me. I am struck to see, on the other hand, how so many ideologies, which fill the world today and rise up against faith, operate in a nonhistorical fashion, yes, as ideologies.

Everything is historical. What we call revelation is a history in which God acted. For all that has happened in that history, from Abraham to Jesus Christ and to Paul, a sojourn in the Holy Land which I have had several times is a very invigorating

confirmation of the faith. Neither Loisy nor Bultmann has ever
been to Palestine. However, that would have brought them
something. Bultmann might have found evidence of a history
that does not contradict itself, but bases in reality its idea of
faith as personal existential decision. In history, everything is
marked by the peculiarity of a moment in space and time, with
cultural and social conditionings. But to recognize that affords
an answer to many difficulties by placing them in their frame
of relativity.

Together with theology and history, it is the liturgy that has
nourished my faith. By my encounter with the Benedictine
monastic life in 1919, I had the grace to be reborn Christianly
in the liturgy. This must be understood, not as ceremony and
ritualism, but as a form of life. Precisely, it is the respiration
of the church. I have lived and still live in the liturgy (notwith-
standing the impoverishment brought about by its present
reform) as the place of my soul's dilation. It is, of course, the
daily Eucharist. It is the cycle of feasts that makes us celebrate,
in the time of seasons and days, the history of the redemption.
It is the daily recitation of the psalms. Without the psalms, I
do not know where I would be. I would, no doubt, have lost
courage. The psalms are the cry of the people of God who,
through all circumstances—sometimes of extreme peril, sometimes of joyous praise, sometimes of simple and very ordinary
service of God in faithfulness—have said and repeated: "You
are my God, you will always be my God." The psalms are the
songs of hope and faithfulness. I have espoused them as the
expression of my soul.

My faith has known a certain evolution, if I consider the
great aspects of it that have dominated my knowledge of God.
I have come rather late to give to the person of Jesus Christ
the central place that he occupies today in my thought and in
my life. As a young seminarian, a young religious, I was rather
seized by "God." Today, after forty-three years of priesthood,
forty-eight years of religious life, after having reflected and
preached much, I believe I have approached a Pauline attitude
in which I ask myself in vain if faith is theocentric or Christo-

centric. "God" is absolutely first, but he is "the Father of Jesus Christ, our Lord" and he is revealed in Jesus Christ. If I dare use such great words for things that are manifest in me in such a mediocre way, it is Jesus Christ who gives light, warmth, and, by his Holy Spirit, movement to my life as I try to live it among men, with them, and for them. Each day he speaks to me. Each day he prevents me from stopping. His gospel and his example snatch me from the instinctive tendency that would keep me bound to myself, to my habits, to my egoism.

I said, "by his Holy Spirit." I was always interested in the Holy Spirit and the bibliography of my publications testifies to this. For about twelve years, however, there has been more than interest. I realize—not only theologically but in living day by day—that it is by the Holy Spirit that what God gives truly becomes reality in us. Is it not the very movement of revelation or of the history of salvation? Has there not been at first the sovereignty of the living God, then the incarnation, then Pentecost? Thus the mission of the Word must be consummated by a coming of the Spirit. It is the Spirit who puts unceasingly before us through the course of days and events the gift of the gospel and of grace that God has given us, once for all, in Jesus Christ. So I must constantly actualize and vivify this gift by calling upon the Holy Spirit and opening my life to his coming. For this, I do not have to join a Pentecostal group, although the charismatic movement (I do not care much for this name) interests me. I like it. But I must confess that an experience has made me more attentive to the criticisms that can be brought against it. But the tree will be judged by its fruits. I am, in any case, extremely reticent before the oversimplification of certain actual movements of revivalism under the sign of "Jesus."

Faith is not rational, but it is reasonable. It is situated above the demonstrable, the scientific. It brings into play other faculties. But it is the reality of men who do not renounce their duty to act reasonably, and who are invited to love and serve God not only with their whole heart but with their whole strength and their whole mind. So I do not reject the contributions of reason. I admit that the "proofs of the existence of God" are more difficult to handle today, but I do not agree with those who cast them wholesale overboard after giving them a fairly casual consideration. It is true that faith is of another category. I like the word of Luther: "The vault of heaven holds up without pillars." But if pillars are given to us, let us not demolish them! One of my old teachers used to say, "Say nothing bad about reason, it is still the best thing we have." The "best"? We could discuss that; but the good, who could deny it?

The Creed begins with God and finishes with eternal life, that is to say, on the object of a hope. My faith is also hope, and hope of that "absolute future" promised to the world. The seed of this hope has been sowed by Jesus Christ through his resurrection.

Lewis A. Drummond

LEWIS A. DRUMMOND WAS BORN IN DIXON, ILLINOIS, in 1926. He is a graduate of Samford University in Birmingham, Alabama, and holds the B.D. and Th.M. degrees from Southwestern Baptist Theological Seminary in Fort Worth, Texas, and the Ph.D. from King's College, University of London.

He has been pastor of Baptist congregations in Columbiana, Alabama; Fort Worth, Texas; Granbury, Texas; Birmingham, Alabama; and Louisville, Kentucky. He was professor of evangelism and pastoral theology in Spurgeon's College, London, and is currently serving as the Billy Graham Associate Professor of Evangelism at the Southern Baptist Theological Seminary in Louisville, Kentucky.

In addition to service on various convention-wide evangelism and stewardship committees in the United States and Britain, he has lectured widely on these subjects both in the States and abroad. His writing appears frequently in popular religious journals; however, scholarly articles have been published in the *Journal of the Victorian Institute*, the *Baptist Theological Quarterly*, and the *Scottish Journal of Theology*. His books include *Evangelism: The Counter Revolution*, *Life Can Be Real*, and *What the Bible Says*, a rewriting of R. A. Torrey's *What the Bible Teaches*. He was also editor of a collection entitled *Sermons from Behind the Iron Curtain*.

Real Life
Is Filled with God's Life

LEWIS A. DRUMMOND

"I WILL STAY UP UNTIL I AM ASSURED THAT I HAVE BEEN FILLED with the Holy Spirit, even if it takes all night." It was at my wife's home during a vacation time when I made that resolve. Already it was late and the rest of the family had gone to bed. This issue had been brewing in my spiritual life for some time. Now the crisis had come! I was alone with God and determined to get the matter settled once and for all—and at any cost.

A Long Spiritual Journey

Many factors and providential experiences had brought me to this critical point. I can now look back over the years and recall numerous incidents in which God was at work leading me to my crisis hour.

I remember very well, as a young Christian in the Armed Forces, meeting one day a high school friend who to my surprise was stationed at the same air base as I. Being eager to share with this friend my newfound faith in Christ, I determined to go to his barracks and witness to him. As I was reading my Bible and praying for God's help to win him, I happened upon John 14:23, where Jesus said: "If a man loves me, he will keep my word, and my Father will love him, and we will come to him and make our home with him."

I may not have understood the verse in the best exegetical sense, but I felt I must pray for God to come to me and make his "home" with me in an unusual way if I were to speak

44

effectively for the Lord Jesus Christ. Somehow God met that sincere request. I knew he had come to me to prepare me for witnessing. So immediately I made my way to my friend's barracks. There I found him and simply told him what Christ had done for me and that the Lord Jesus would do the same for him. That God was at work in the entire experience was verified for me when a day or two later my friend said he had been praying ever since our conversation that Christ would become his Savior. I understood little or nothing at that time of what it meant to be "filled with the Spirit." But God had met a special need in my life as I prayed for his power. Moreover, a process had begun which moved on to its climax on that night at my wife's home.

A few years later, when I was in college, I spoke one evening to a small Christian house group. At that time I had not received a call to preach, but I was always eager to share Christ whenever I could. In the group that night was a lady I much admired. She had been a cripple for many years, but the dynamic winsomeness of her Christian life was contagious to all. Everyone deeply appreciated her. After I had finished speaking, she said something that shocked me. I remember it very vividly, though the incident was sometime ago. She graciously complimented me on my message and then said: "I believe this young man has experienced the same thing as I have. I believe he has been filled with the Holy Spirit." I did not quite know how to react or what to make out of it. Yet it strangely moved me. What does it mean to be Spirit-filled? I wondered. God was leading me to my crisis point.

After becoming convinced that the ministry was God's will for my life, I started preaching. One summer two of my college friends and I conducted several evangelistic campaigns. Before I left for these meetings a book on the Spirit-filled life fell into my hands. It was a small, simple volume dealing with the rudiments of the concept. I do not even remember now how I acquired the book. But I took it along with me. If this book can help me learn how to possess more power in witnessing, I thought, I will surely read it. I distinctly remember reading through its pages one day and being made aware that there are definite requirements in order to be filled with God's Spirit. Moreover, I discovered that there are definite disciplines if we are to remain in that spiritual state. Another step in the process was taken. God was still working in my life.

College days came to an end. I married and went to seminary. God blessed our lives, and I became pastor of a small new church near the campus. All the time God was revealing to me more and more of the truth of what it means to live a life of power, "filled with all the fulness of God" (Eph. 3:19). I started praying very definitely that God would send the power of his Holy Spirit upon my preaching. Then one day I met a young preacher. I could tell that this man had a deep living experience of God. We had prayer together, and I never heard anyone pray quite like he did. It was obvious this man knew the Lord Jesus in a most unusual way. We became close friends and spent many hours together. He taught me more in those hours about the Spirit-filled life than I had ever imagined possible. God spoke to me profoundly through this man. The Holy Spirit was clearly continuing to lead.

Finally, I got hold of a book by R. A. Torrey. This scholarly author has written much on the theme of the Holy Spirit. In his work *The Holy Spirit: Who He Is and What He Does,* Torrey sets out in analytical style the entire concept of the Spirit-filled life. It was as I was reading this volume that God precipitated my night of crisis. Between seminary terms, my wife and I had traveled to her home. I had been reading Torrey's book and now the hour came when God seemed to be saying to me: "This is the moment of truth for you. This is your hour to have the full assurance that you are living and serving me in the fullness of my Holy Spirit." I had thought, prayed, discussed, and read about the theme for months—even years. But now I knew that I must be assured that the experience was mine. I was determined. I would not go to bed until I knew I was filled with the Spirit. I wanted—at any cost—my life to be real.

Is It Real?

Is such a spiritual attitude and exercise defensible, however? Is it not too subjective and mystical? These are the questions I had to answer. I had to admit that such an approach to the Christian life is feasible only if it can be shown undeniably that there actually is an experience of being filled with the Spirit of God.

Some Personal Testimonies

Yet, great men of God through the ages give testimony to the experience. A sweep of church history shows the idea constantly reasserting itself. The early church fathers—Origen, Jerome, Ambrose, and others—talk much of the work of the Holy Spirit in the life of the believer. As the years of God's dealings with men unfolded, giants of the Christian faith constantly emphasized the need. Men like Savonarola, Fénelon, George Fox, John Bunyan, Wesley, and Whitefield give testimony to the necessity of being rightly related to the Holy Spirit of God.

The past century saw a fresh emphasis upon the theme. It was D. L. Moody, a great nineteenth-century evangelist, who said:

The blessing came upon me suddenly like a flash of lightning. For months I had been hungering and thirsting for power in service. I had come to that point where I think I would have died if I had not got it. I remember I was walking the streets of New York. I had no more heart in the business I was about than if I had not been in the world at all. Well, one day—oh, what a day! I cannot describe it, I seldom refer to it, it is almost too sacred an experience to name—right there on the streets the power of God seemed to come upon me so wonderfully I had to ask God to stay his hand. I was filled with a sense of God's goodness and I felt as though I could take the whole world to my heart. I took the old sermons I had preached before without any power, it was the same old truth, but there was new power. Many were impressed and converted. This happened years after

I was converted myself. I would not now be placed back where I was before that blessed experience if you should give me all the world—it would be as the small dust in the balance.

Charles G. Finney, America's great revivalist, stated:

I was powerfully converted on the morning of the tenth of October, 1821. In the evening of the same day I received overwhelming baptisms of the Holy Ghost, that went through, as it seemed to me, body and soul. I immediately found myself endued with such power from on high that a few words dropped here and there to individuals were the means of their immediate conversion.

R. A. Torrey, Bible teacher and preacher, gives his testimony in these words:

I was led to seek the baptism of the Holy Spirit because I became convinced from the study of The Acts of the Apostles that no one had a right to preach the gospel until he had been baptized with the Holy Spirit. At last I was led to the place where I said that I would never enter the pulpit again until I had been baptized with the Holy Ghost and knew it or until God showed me in some way to do it.

C. H. Spurgeon, probably the greatest of all Victorian preachers, one day quoted in a sermon Luke 11:13 where Jesus said, "If you then, who are evil, know how to give good gifts to your children, how much more will the heavenly Father give the Holy Spirit to those who *ask* him?" Spurgeon then cried out: "Oh, let us ask him at once, with all our hearts. Am I not so happy as to have in this audience some who will immediately ask? You that are the children of God—to you is this promise especially made. Ask God to make you all that the Spirit of God can make you, not only a satisfied believer who has drunk for himself but a useful believer who overflows the neighborhood with blessing."

And it is not just the nineteenth-century men who stressed this truth. Many in our contemporary scene are urging Christians to seek such a blessing. I will never forget hearing Dr.

Forrest Feazer at a large Texas rally preaching on the subject of the Spirit-filled life. At the climax of his message he said in essence: "I do not care what you call it; the infilling, the baptism, the second blessing, or what have you. The issue is, have you experienced it?"

The Bible Answer

It becomes clear that God's great men give their assent and commitment to the idea. But above all, one must turn to the Word of God for the ultimate answer. I have always held that the Bible is the final court of appeal. In looking to the Bible for help on the validity of the Spirit-filled life, we are naturally drawn to The Acts of the Apostles. Here we find much emphasis laid on the Spirit's work; and that from a quite practical perspective. In Acts, ch. 2, there is a graphic account of the miraculous giving of the Holy Spirit on the Day of Pentecost.

To understand clearly what precipitated this historic event, we must turn back to the third Gospel where Luke, who is also the author of Acts, tells us that the Lord Jesus Christ commissioned his disciples to proclaim the good news to nothing less than the entire world (Luke 24:45–48). This is a staggering commission. How could a mere handful of men and women of such limited resources possibly accomplish such a herculean task?

But then Jesus said to his newly commissioned followers, "I send the promise of my Father upon you; but stay in the city, until you are clothed with power from on high" (Luke 24:49). Now the situation was suddenly changed. The task *could* be fulfilled. They were to go back into Jerusalem and there wait on the Lord, for in a few days they would be equipped by God himself in order that they might fill their role in world evangelization. They would soon be "clothed with power from on high." And when that happened, nothing could defeat them as they went out to share Christ. Ten days later, Jesus kept his promise, and we read:

When the day of Pentecost had come, they were all together
in one place. And suddenly a sound came from heaven like the
rush of a mighty wind, and it filled all the house where they were
sitting. And there appeared to them tongues as of fire, dis-
tributed and resting on each one of them. And they were all
filled with the Holy Spirit and began to speak in other tongues,
as the Spirit gave them utterance. (Acts 2:1–4.)

Many things could—and perhaps should—be said about this
important passage. But for our present purposes, we must
confine ourselves to observing only two vital issues.

First, on the Day of Pentecost all the believers in the Lord
Jesus Christ received the Holy Spirit as God's gift. Every time
a person puts his faith in Jesus Christ, he immediately receives
the gift of the Spirit. This is why Paul told the believers in
Corinth that their bodies were the temple of God (I Cor. 6:19).
No one is excepted. God's gift of the Spirit is for all Christians.

Secondly, these early believers not only received the Holy
Spirit for the first time; they were also *filled* with God's Spirit.
As a great scholar stated, these first followers of Christ had "a
reception from the Spirit of extraordinary powers, in addition
to sanctifying grace." In a word, they received the Spirit and
were filled with the Spirit simultaneously.

Of course, this particular passage should not be pushed too
far as an illustration of this basic truth. Pentecost was unique.
This was the hour for God to pour out his Spirit "on all flesh"
(Acts 2:17). This was the moment when the Holy Spirit *first*
came to dwell in all believers. It was a tremendous epic in the
life of the church. In that sense it is unrepeatable. At the same
time, however, the passage surely implies that a Christian is to
have a deeper experience of the Holy Spirit than merely knowing that Christ lives in his life. Christians are to be conscious
of the Holy Spirit's *infilling*. Surely Pentecost tells us that.

Other Accounts of Infillings

In Acts 4:31 we read, "And when they had prayed, the place
in which they were gathered together was shaken; and they

were all filled with the Holy Spirit and spoke the word of God
with boldness." Here Luke tells us that the same disciples who
had shared in Pentecost again experienced an infilling of the
Holy Spirit. Persecution had come to the infant church. They
gathered together to pray for boldness to communicate their
message. And God marvelously met their need by filling them
with the Spirit.

Or take the experience of Paul in that interesting account
found in Acts, ch. 19. Here Paul met some people in Ephesus
whom he assumed to be believers, but he perhaps sensed that
something was wrong. So he asked them, "Did you receive the
Holy Spirit when you believed?" (v. 2a). They answered, "We
have never even heard that there is a Holy Spirit" (v. 2b). This
somewhat shocked the apostle and caused him to ask further,
"Into what then were you baptized?" (v. 3). They then told
Paul they had only received John's baptism. So Paul instructed
them more fully about Christ, baptized them, laid his hands
upon them and "the Holy Spirit came upon them" (v. 6).

Paul was much concerned that these new converts were fully
instructed on the issues involved with the inner work of the
Holy Spirit. Moreover, he probably saw the gift of the Spirit
and all his fullness as an experience taking place simultaneously
with conversion. Actually, this is the way it should be. This
approach would obviously solve many of the problems that new
converts have regarding spiritual growth.

Paul's letter to the Ephesians forcefully brings home the
necessity of being Spirit-filled as he says, "Do not get drunk
with wine, for that is debauchery; but be filled with the Spirit"
(Eph. 5:18). Paul fully expected the Ephesian believers to live
lives filled with the Spirit of God. It was not left as optional.
It was not to be approached casually or only if it aroused
interest. The force of the verse is in the imperative: "You must
be filled" with the Spirit. It is a positive command, just as the
first part of the verse is a negative command against drunken-
ness.

Naturally, Jesus himself lived out his entire ministry in the
fullness of the Spirit. All he said and did was directed by and

permeated with the Holy Spirit. This is reiterated over and over in the Gospels. Now if Christ is our example in all things —and surely he is—then we are to emulate him in this relationship to the Holy Spirit. Thus the Spirit-filled life is clearly mandatory for us.

Space forbids going into the numerous other New Testament passages that teach this same essential truth. Thus if we take the Bible seriously, we cannot sidestep the fact that God's intention for all his people is that they become Spirit-filled Christians.

How It Happens

After being convinced of the validity of the whole idea, how do I come to him to be filled? Let me give five simple principles that helped me tremendously in my quest for God's fullness. They are the essence of the exercise I went through that night when I first determined I would become a Spirit-filled Christian and of that which I now experience daily.

Acknowledgment. First, there must be an *acknowledgment* of need. If we are satisfied with the present state of our spiritual life, then little else will happen. But remember the words of the Lord Jesus when he said, "Blessed are those who hunger and thirst for righteousness, for they shall be satisfied" (Matt. 5:6). If we have not a real hunger for all that God has for us, we should earnestly ask him to inspire such a desire in us. Surely there is much to move us in that direction. There are tragic needs all over the world that should be met in Christ's name. We cannot even begin to meet these needs in our own strength; we need God's power.

There is also the desire that life be full and meaningful. And surely we have learned now that life is real only when it is filled with God's life. Actually, the Spirit-filled life is what life is all about.

Then, above all, our deepest desire is to glorify our Lord Jesus Christ. And he is glorified the most when he can possess us and fill us with all of himself. Thus, there should be that within us which cries out for the fullness of God. Moreover, the Holy Spirit himself will help create that hunger. May God bring us all to that attitude of the psalmist when he said: "As a hart longs for flowing streams, so longs my soul for thee, O God. My soul thirsts for God, for the living God" (Ps. 42:1–2).

Abandonment. Granted that we have something of a genuine desire for God's best and have acknowledged our need, we next must *abandon* our sins. The Scriptures are very explicit as to how sin disrupts the work of the Spirit in our lives. The Bible tells us we can resist him (Acts 7:51), grieve him (Eph. 4:30), and quench him (I Thess. 5:19). When we thus sin we shall never know his infilling. In reality, we must make a 100 percent break with all known sin. Now it is not sinless perfection we are asking for. We all have unknown sins in our lives and we can hardly confess these by name. But we can make a break with every *known* evil. We must strive to be able to say with Paul, "So I always take pains to have a clear conscience toward God and toward men" (Acts 24:16).

I was once preaching on this theme in a church where I served as pastor. A young man came to me and said: "Pastor, you are preaching too hard to the people. It is expecting too much to ask for a 100 percent break with all known sin." But is this asking too much? I think not. Sin, unforsaken and unconfessed, severs our fellowship with God. We cannot have Christ's fullness in one hand and grasp sin in the other.

Abdication. Next, we must *abdicate* the throne of our heart. In the final analysis, we are faced with this issue: will I control my own self or will I truly make Jesus the Lord of my life? It has to be one or the other. God's word is very plain on this point. In Acts we read that the Holy Spirit is given to "those who obey him" (Acts 5:32). Jesus must be made Lord. God wants our complete obedience. We must become his subjects to do, go, speak, act, and live as he wishes. In a figure, we are to give up the chairmanship of the board in our life, move out from the head of the conference table and become a junior executive. Jesus must become "chairman."

I suppose we are often somewhat fearful of doing this lest

we become less of a person. But nothing could be farther from the truth. Actually, we become a real person only when we yield to Jesus Christ. We are only truly "free" as the Son of God makes us free (John 8:36). Or it may be that we fear that God will ask some terrible thing of us if we yield ourselves to him. But remember, he is a Father. He loves us. He wants only the best for us. His will is always that which brings fulfillment and meaning to life.

Asking. Fourthly, after acknowledging our need, abandoning our sin, and abdicating control of our lives, we simply *ask* God to fill us with his Spirit. "If you then, who are evil, know how to give good gifts to your children, how much more will the heavenly Father give the Holy Spirit to those who ask him!" (Luke 11:13). God deeply desires us to come into his presence by prayer and ask him for this gift. This is obviously the essence of the crisis moment. Having paid the price mentioned above, we are now ready to ask. And when we ask, we may be assured that God is ready to listen and do as he promised.

Accepting. Finally, having asked, we now must *accept* the gift by faith and thank God for his goodness. We just accept by faith what God has promised. We accept salvation by faith; so also we claim by faith the infilling of his Spirit.

I must admit it took me some time to see this. Really, this is what kept me up late at night when my first crisis hour came. I suppose I was expecting some certain manifestation. Most of us find it a bit difficult to claim by faith alone God's promise of the Spirit. We all tend to feel that we must have the same kind of experience someone else has had. I prayed and prayed. I felt that I had paid the price. I was hungry for all God had. I wanted my life to be real. So I kept asking and asking God to fill me. Finally, I saw the principle that if I had done my part, God will surely do his. He keeps his word. He is faithful. Suddenly that broke in on me. So I just accepted it as an accomplished fact. I saw that the transaction was complete. I thanked God for filling me with his blessed Spirit, and went to bed. And you can do the same.

William H. DuBay

WILLIAM H. DuBAY RECEIVED HIS B.A. IN PHILOSO-
phy at St. John's College in Camarillo, California, and
was ordained to the Roman Catholic priesthood in
1960. In the middle sixties he called upon Pope Paul
VI to remove James Cardinal McIntyre from office for
his alleged failures in dealing with the civil rights
issues of the time.

In 1966 Father DuBay published a book entitled
The Human Church, in which he called upon the
church to expend its human resources in solving human problems. Following the publication of this work,
he was suspended from the priesthood. He has continued to be active in humanitarian causes, serving as
consultant to Synanon and director of the VISTA
Training Program in California. He was instrumental
in founding Stonewall, a group home for homosexuals
and other sexual minorities.

He has continued to speak and write on various
aspects of the crisis of religion and social change. His
articles have appeared in *America, Changing Education, Christianity Today, Commonweal, McCalls
Magazine,* and *The Saturday Evening Post.*

Faith Is Always New

WILLIAM H. DuBAY

I FIND MY FAITH BECOMING MORE AND MORE MONOTHEISTIC. For one thing, I have come to reject the devil worship in Christianity. Except for the Satanic cults, no one seems to give belief in the devil and the concept of evil more credibility than Christians. Remarking about the rise of popularity of Satanism recently, the pope as much as said, "See, we told you there was a devil!"

This is more than a symbiotic interdependence of two conflicting beliefs—such as atheism and faith. It is also a leftover of the polytheism of our ancient Hebrew past. There was a time, I suppose, when the Lord of the Flies, Beelzebub, had a more savory reputation among the hearth gods of the Middle East. It was the contribution of the Hebrew prophets to bring him down a niche or two. But that was the problem, he was never fully deposed, at least in the mind of the church.

He was to remain a rival of God, his enemy and competitor for the souls of men. A great amount of energy was spent by Christian evangelists, in fact, in the description of this conflict and the final outcome. Christian salvation was always cast in the framework of that great cosmic war. This made for good sermons, and very good theology, really, but very poor metaphysics.

For one thing, it took a lot of the control of the universe out of the hands of God. The conflict described in the catechism and in sermons was a real one, and not make-believe. This meant that one could never be quite sure about the outcome, the devil wielded a lot of power, and even held most of the earth in his captivity. This makes God something less than a god, a no-god, for my money. Either God is in perfect control —without rival, worry, or conflict—or he is no god at all, and we have to look someplace else for one. This is what I have been doing.

Which leads us to the next step. Without a devil to pester us and mess things up, there is no need for evil. If our God is a perfect god, he can't afford to make even one mistake. If God made a mistake, then we are all in a lot of trouble. Either the universe is going exactly the way he wants it, or there is no god. This leads us to the conclusion that we are living in the best of all possible worlds, a perfect world, really, with only our blindness and lack of insight preventing us from enjoying its perfection—and a lot of ancient myths about evil that were useful for purposes of social control but not much help in attaining happiness.

The devil and evil myths did little to advance man's moral progress. They provide the basic framework for intolerance. As long as the world is divided into two warring camps, there will always be the tendency to divide people into the saved and the damned, the good and the evil, the baptized and the infidels (and to put into those categories the blacks and the whites, the gays and the straights, the communists and us, the males and the females).

Now, if we are living in the best of all possible worlds, then there is really no need for heaven. We are all already there. It is just a simple matter of putting those things such as pain, suffering, and death into the context of a perfect world, a heavenly one, and that is not difficult.

If we look around us and look deeply, we can see that nature does not make mistakes. And, contrary to our Western myth about progress (things are getting better and better), we can see that nature is not proceeding in an evolutionary, straight-line development. The universe did not start out imperfect and undeveloped; its perfection was here to begin with. There is no superfluity, no waste in nature, but a perfect economy of re-

sources, a perfect balance of energies. Science has shown us a
universe that is much more perfect than the Bible ever promised. The universe is not getting better, only changing, always
making the right choices, never having to correct a mistake—
there is no such thing. Man is a thinking, loving, warm being
because he is part of a warm, thinking, and loving universe. He
is not an intellectual fluke floating about a cold and hostile
universe, waiting to be released from his entrapment.

For centuries the church kept a whole continent of people
on the verge of lunacy with its lies about evil. Mental hospitals
and waiting rooms are still packed with the victims of that
dichotomous view that divides reality into good and bad and
structures one's life on paranoia. What joy there is in discover-
ing that God is good, that he has placed us in a paradise, and
there is never the need for fear!

Augustine said that the only sin the church can commit is
not to preach the gospel. It has been a long time since the
church has preached a good word of salvation to the world. It
has been mostly damnation to the world. Jesus said he saw
Satan fall like lightning from heaven. That is a lesson the
church never learned. Christians have to realize that to declare
the death of the devil is not to declare the death of God, but
his perfection, and the perfection of his works.

Avery Dulles

Avery Dulles was born in Auburn, New York, in 1918. He was graduated from Harvard College and studied law at Harvard before entering the U.S. Naval Reserve in which he served in the Caribbean and Mediterranean areas. He entered the novitiate of the Society of Jesus at Poughkeepsie, New York, earning the S.T.L. degree at Woodstock College and the S.T.D. at Pontifical Gregorian University in Rome.

Father Dulles has taught at Fordham University and at present he is professor of systematic theology at Woodstock College. He has been guest lecturer at Union Theological Seminary in New York, at Princeton Theological Seminary, and at Pontifical Gregorian University in Rome. Among his many responsibilities, he is a member of the Catholic Bishops' Advisory Council, Consultor to the Papal Secretariat for Dialogue with Non-Believers, and a member of the American Theological Society. He holds the Croix de Guerre, and is a member of Phi Beta Kappa.

Among his many writings, mostly in the theological and apologetics fields, his *Apologetics and the Biblical Christ* has been translated into French, Korean, and Polish. He received the Christopher award for his book *The Survival of Dogma. A Testimonial to Grace* has been translated into Italian and Spanish; *Spirit, Faith, and Church*, written in collaboration with Wolfhart Pannenberg and Carl E. Braaten, has been translated into German.

An Unfolding Process

AVERY DULLES

I BECAME A CHRISTIAN, A CATHOLIC, A THEOLOGIAN, AND A lover of history all as parts of one and the same process. During my undergraduate days at college, in the late 1930's, I was won over by Augustine, by Thomas Aquinas, by Dante, and by the medieval cathedrals. I felt that any faith which had given rise to so much beauty and wisdom—beautiful wisdom and wise beauty—must contain more than enough to nourish a hungry seeker like myself.

My turn to Christian faith in a highly dogmatic—and perhaps anachronistic—form was in part a revolt against the emptiness of the modern world. I was little attracted by the noisy entertainments and the superficial consumerism of contemporary American society. Although I would not have wanted to live in the thirteenth century, I admired the quality of its achievements.

Through medieval culture I found my way back to its sources —Greek wisdom and the Gospels. In both I discovered a vivid appreciation of the invisible and the transcendent.

From Plato in particular I learned to distrust outward appearances and to esteem thoughtful inquiry into goals and ideals. His vision of the "idea of the good" as the summit of all reality and his esteem for virtue as the true good of man caused me to look on the world with new eyes. If Plato had taught me nothing else, I should be forever indebted to him for having convinced me that it is better to suffer—even to the point of losing one's life—than to commit injustice. The evil that we suffer at the hands of others does not touch the inmost reality which makes us what we truly are. The evil that we do, however, makes us inwardly rotten and corrupt. Is that not what Christ also taught in the Gospels?

Nietzsche once described Christianity as the Platonism of the masses. He intended this description to be contemptuous, but in his mockery he called attention to a profound truth. For all the contrasts that can be drawn between Platonism and Christianity, the similarities are to my mind even more striking. In reading the New Testament, I have often been struck by what might be called the Platonism of the Sermon on the Mount. The Beatitudes express in vivid, hyperbolic language the blessedness of those who aspire only to the divine goal of justice. What does it profit a man, Jesus asks elsewhere, to gain the whole world if he suffers the loss of his own soul? Although both Paul and John thought in primarily Semitic categories, there is something Platonistic in Paul's contrast between the spirit and the flesh and in John's doctrine of the divine Logos.

Reading the Gospels in my college days, I conceived a desire to subordinate everything to following Jesus. I was prepared to give up everything else for the pearl of great price, to sell all that I possessed for the sake of the buried treasure in the field (Matt. 13:44–45). I was drawn particularly by the austere, demanding Jesus of Matthew's Gospel, and wished that I could hear directly what he would ask of me.

An essential element in the Gospel, as I came to understand it, was the continued presence of Jesus in the company of his disciples. Through the church and its pastors, Jesus makes it possible for us to hear him by listening to those who speak in his name. "He who hears you hears me, and he who rejects you rejects me, and he who rejects me rejects him who sent me." (Luke 10:16.) Christianity seems to me to be impossible without an obedient hearing of a living and authoritative voice that speaks in the name of Christ.

I turned to Catholicism partly because the Protestant churches, at least in my experience of them, did not seem to take authority seriously. Some, to be sure, took the Bible seriously, but Jesus, I was convinced, demanded more than attachment to a book. He wanted a living community of faith. Although popes and bishops no doubt have made many mistakes, they have kept alive the authoritative presence of Christ. Better than any other group I could find, they represented in the contemporary world the exigency of the gospel, and the Catholic faithful seemed to be the most disciplined of the large communions. My allegiance to Jesus therefore took me to an authoritative and dogmatic church.

The same movement of faith that made me a Christian and a Catholic later impelled me, at the close of World War II, to enter the Society of Jesus. The founder of the Jesuits, Ignatius of Loyola, appealed to me because of his militant loyalty to the church. Living at the dawn of modern times, he revived something of the evangelical spirit of Francis of Assisi and Saint Dominic. I wanted to join in the effort to keep these medieval ideals alive in the world of our day and to labor, as Jesuits did, in the service of the hierarchical church.

I was ordained to the priesthood in 1956, ten years after entering the Society of Jesus. After completing my doctoral studies in Rome, I began to teach theology in 1960. Since that time, my theological attitudes and interests have been gradually changing. I have continued to be concerned with authority, but I have come to understand it in a more nuanced way. This is true for several reasons.

For one thing, I have been increasingly impressed by the poverty of human concepts and language in comparison with the greatness and majesty of God. Human formulas often serve as pointers that help to focus and intensify our sense of God, but they do not afford definitions that enable us to put the divine into clear categories. Many of the best confessional formulas are negative in character, for, as Thomas Aquinas said, we can say more accurately what God is not than what he is.

Secondly, I have felt a deepening awareness of the historical and cultural limitations in all human formulations of the faith. As I have tried to use ancient documents to throw light on contemporary discussions, I have come to see that each age has its own situation and its own task. The task of reexpressing the faith so as to meet the presuppositions, concerns, and thought categories of a given period is an unending challenge.

Vatican Council II, reacting against certain exaggerations in counterreformation Catholicism, sought to foster a keener realization of both the mystery of God and the historicity of man. It consequently supplied a corrective to the tendency of Catholics, in recent centuries, to repeat mechanically the formulas handed down in Scripture and by tradition. In its effort to meet the current crisis of authority, Vatican II challenged Catholics to become more adventurous and creative; and this challenge has proved no easy one to meet. As a Jesuit theologian, I consider it one of my chief tasks to help the church to follow the Council's initiatives by involving itself more with the problems of the modern world.

Because of the changes in my point of view, paralleling the developments canonized by Vatican II, I find it hard to state in precise language exactly what one ought to think about many of the traditional Christian themes, such as God, Christ, and immortality. The center of Christian faith, I would hold, is that self-revelation which God made in the life, death, and resurrection of Jesus. But this revelation comes differently to each of us, depending on where we are. We have to keep asking ourselves what we think of Christ in his meaning for our particular world, with all its joys, hopes, fears, and sufferings. If we do not confront our own world but remain merely on the plane of abstract formulas, we have not really apprehended the revelation of God in Christ.

Faith, therefore, seems to me less a set of hard-and-fast answers than a constantly unfolding process. The process, of course, is shaped by one's prior convictions about where truth is to be found, but the process itself, if fruitfully carried on, tends to modify one's convictions. Any affirmations I might make today about the content of my faith could in theory be changed by the results of further inquiry. But this does not mean that I have no firm convictions. On the contrary, every-

thing that I have found through inquiry makes me more attached than previously to the fundamental articles of Christian
belief.

I am in sympathy with the efforts of some German and
Dutch theologians, generally called "liberals," to find new ways
of thinking and speaking about traditional doctrines such as
creation, original sin, the incarnation, the resurrection, and the
Eucharist. On the other hand, I am very much on guard against
changes that would weaken or dilute the Christian message. To
me God's revelation in Christ is distinctive and unique. Thus
I am unwilling to settle for any view that would reduce Jesus
to the stature of our common humanity (eliminating his
divinity), that would interpret his resurrection as a merely
psychological occurrence in the lives of the disciples, or that
would trivialize the real presence of Christ in the Lord's Supper. The doctrinal changes that appeal to me are those which
increase the power of the gospel to speak to the modern world,
those which give the Christian revelation greater relevance and
impact.

Augustine once said: Seek in order that you may find, and
find in order to seek yet more. From 1940 to 1960 I sought
primarily in order to find. Having found so much, I have felt
impelled, since 1960, to be an inquirer once again—an inquirer
not from outside but from inside the commitment of faith. In
this quest I believe that I am following the lead of the Holy
Spirit, who is at work not in me alone but in the entire community of believers. I feel more than ever united to the church as
a pilgrim people that incessantly meditates on its own heritage
of faith. To resist this process of reexamination and growth,
whether from fear or lack of interest, would be, in my opinion,
to bury one's talents in a napkin rather than to put them to
work for the glory of God (cf. Matt. 25:14–30). By probing
restlessly into the mystery of Christ, the church, I believe,
advances "to mature manhood, to the measure of the stature
of the fulness of Christ" (Eph. 4:13).

It has been a privilege, in the past several decades, to be
constantly laboring on the frontiers of faith, and thus to make

some small contribution to the church's ongoing reflection on the meaning of its vocation. I treasure my own calling as a theologian because it has focused my attention on those issues which give meaning and greatness to human life.

Georgia Harkness

GEORGIA HARKNESS WAS BORN ON A FARM NEAR Harkness, New York, in 1898. She attended Cornell University, and received her M.A., M.R.E., and Ph.D. degrees from Boston University. She also studied at Harvard, Yale, and Union Theological Seminary in New York.

Her early teaching experience was at the Boston University School of Religious Education, Elmira College, and Mount Holyoke College. From 1939 until 1950 she was associate professor of applied theology at Garrett Theological Seminary in Evanston, Illinois, and held a similar post until 1961 at the Pacific School of Religion in Berkeley, California. She also taught at the Japan Christian University.

Ordained to the ministry in the Methodist Church in 1926, and appointed to a seminary faculty in 1939, she was a forerunner of women's liberation. She received a Scroll of Honor award in 1941 from the General Federation of Women's Clubs for "pioneer work in religion." She was a delegate to the Oxford Conference in 1937, the Madras Conference in 1938, the organizing assembly of the World Council of Churches in Amsterdam in 1948, the Lund Conference in 1952, and the Evanston Assembly in 1954. She was the author of thirty-five books.

The death of Georgia Harkness occurred while this book was being edited.

Faith Is for Living

GEORGIA HARKNESS

I AM GLAD TO BE ASKED TO GIVE A WITNESS TO MY PERSONAL Christian faith. It has long been my conviction that theologians by profession should also try to be persons with a commitment to the faith they teach, speak, and write about. This is not to say that I, or any other person, can fully measure up to the high demands of God's revelation in Christ. We all need to remember, as *The Imitation of Christ* enjoins us, "Thou art a man and not God, thou art flesh and no angel." (Part III, Chapter 62.) Yet we can set before us the goal of being a man or a woman of God, and such a commitment is required of us.

It is also my conviction that all theology must be "applied theology," in a measure, and in ways which each theologian must find for himself. It must be workable theology, applicable to life. There is a place for theologizing that probes the concepts and employs the diction appropriate to the higher echelons of the profession, as there is advanced research and technical terminology in every field. Yet since Christian faith relates essentially to God's encounter with persons in the processes of human living, its concepts and terms ought to be translatable into language that any person of ordinary intelligence can understand. This is why I have made a lifelong effort in my teaching and writing to use as simple diction as I could without oversimplifying the issues. None of us will unravel all the mysteries of God, but in communicating the faith we have, we ought not to create more mysteries. This belief is also the reason why, when I began my eleven years of teaching at

Garrett Theological Seminary, I chose to receive the title, not of Systematic Theology as was customary, but of Applied Theology. This designation was then retained when I subsequently taught another eleven years at the Pacific School of Religion.

The term "faith" is used ambiguously. It can mean something beyond human knowledge that must be accepted without sufficient evidence to prove it. In some contexts this is what faith is, and the author of the Letter to the Hebrews stated it in a classic definition: "Now faith is the assurance of things hoped for, the conviction of things not seen" (Heb. 11:1). But faith need not be that for which there is no evidence, and it is seriously to distort the Christian faith to make it a form of credulity—as is too often done. It is the task of theology to discern the grounds of our faith as far as our minds can take us. Faith, then, becomes *belief*, belief that imparts assurance. The next step is *conviction*, that on which our living is grounded. It is essential that faith in these two senses should cohere with each other if either is to be fully authentic.

A good many years ago I wrote a book, now out of print, with the title *The Faith by Which the Church Lives.* The title was prompted by my serving with others from various lands on the drafting committee for this theme at the Madras Conference of the International Missionary Council in 1938. This brought home to me the need for saying as authentically and yet as simply as possible the basic convictions that have sustained the church all through the centuries, and are as vital today as ever.

In the final chapter of this book I summarized this faith as I saw it—the living faith of the church which I also felt to be my own. Turning back to this statement to see what I wrote so long ago, I find that I still believe these same things, though at some points I should add others. I doubt that I could improve on this statement if I were to attempt another now, so I wish to restate it as my personal faith.

> *I believe in God*—a Being supreme in wisdom, power, and goodness who controls the universe and presides over human destinies. Though any symbol drawn from human personality is

inadequate to describe the fullness of his nature, God is best conceived in terms of personality. Creative power, moral judgment, and redemptive love meet in Jesus' symbol of divine fatherhood.

I believe in man—child of eternity in time. A creature fashioned in God's image, yet unable to be master of himself. Though man is endowed with the gift of moral freedom, his use of it is limited by weakness and corrupted by sin. To the receptive and the penitent, God in gracious love offers forgiveness and power.

I believe in Jesus Christ—friend and teacher, Lord and Saviour, the incarnation of God. In him is both the supreme revelation of God and the supreme gift of God for man's salvation. God has not left himself without a witness among any people, and this presence is to be discerned through nature, through history, through beauty, through human personality, and through the spiritual insights of men of all faiths. Yet in Christ alone is God fully manifest. God has not left us to strive in utter feebleness; he empowers us through our natural endowment and our social heritage to aspire toward the good life and in some measure to achieve it. Yet in Christ alone is the grace of God fully laid hold upon. No man may live without sin; whosoever will may find victory through Christ.

I believe in the Kingdom—the righteous rule of God within the family of God. It is both a divine gift and a human task. It is an invisible and eternal goal; yet its reality is visible in time, manifest in redeemed individuals and in communities transformed by love. It comes upon earth as brotherhood increases; it will come beyond earth as God admits us to a more perfect fellowship with himself.

I believe in the Church—the living body of the indwelling Christ, the worshiping Christian fellowship, the conserver of the gospel and its growing-point in history. It is related to the Kingdom as means to end, and it is the indispensable, though it is not the only, agency for the advancement of the Kingdom. As a visible structure the Church has in many respects fallen short of Christ's true Church. Yet even within the visible Church with all its imperfections we see in the fact of the world Christian community a sign of the coming of the Kingdom.

I believe in the duty of the Christian to bear witness to his faith. The ways in which to do it are infinitely various, and each must find his way. We must do this in a union of tolerance with conviction, of courage with tact, of reticence with boldness, of initiative with willingness to be led. Both prayer and action, both reason and revelation must steadily correct and clarify our witness.

Finally, *I believe in the limitless resources of God for every situation.* This is a day in which to be serious. But it is not a day in which to give up. The Christian heritage of truth and brotherhood is in jeopardy, and only divine power in conjunction with the wisest human effort can preserve it. Yet we know it will not be lost. Both within and beyond this world, the riches of God revealed in Christ will deliver us from evil. The Church has a mission and the capacity to perform it, for the Church has a faith by which it lives. (*Op. cit.,* pp. 158–161.)

The principal notes that I would add to this statement if I were writing now would be an affirmation of my belief in the Holy Spirit and some further words on eternal life. I believe profoundly in the presence of the Holy Spirit, which is the presence of God and also of the living Christ, within our world and our daily living. As one of the modern creeds puts it succinctly but powerfully, "We believe in the Holy Spirit, God present with us for guidance, for comfort, and for strength." Another approaches it from a different angle but to the same effect, "We believe in the Holy Spirit as the divine presence in our lives, whereby we are kept in perpetual remembrance of the truth of Christ, and find strength and help in time of need." (*The Methodist Hymnal,* Parthenon Press, 1964, nos. 740, 741.) Since every time is a time of need, we need always to have a sense of God's nearness and sustaining care. Without belief in the Holy Spirit, prayer as communion with God or as petition for inner strength and guidance would have little meaning. I do not recall, or understand, why the Holy Spirit was not included in the affirmations quoted above. He certainly belongs there.

About eternal life, one must speak, but speak more guard- edly. That there is life beyond death by the goodness and

mercy of God is a Christian conviction of long standing which
I share. About the nature of it, I feel that we must be appropri-
ately reticent, for our eternal destiny is in God's hands. Any
attempt to picture the future life is apt to run into extravagant
and sometimes very this-worldly imagery, and to believe that
God assigns unbelievers to an eternal hell of fire and torment
is unworthy of the God of love whom Jesus presents to us. If
we understand how the Bible came to be written, we do not
need to accept its symbolic imagery as literal description. Yet
to believe that God loves and prizes persons so much that he
does not let their lives be snuffed out by death, and that their
loved ones are safe and happy in his nearer presence—these are
credible beliefs which I do not wish to surrender, nor do I see
any need to do so.

Another strong conviction that I have, presupposed in several of the previous statements though not specifically spelled
out in them, is the call of Christ to be sensitive to human need
wherever it is found. This is God's world in which he loves all
his human children, and we are bidden not only to love God
supremely but our neighbor as ourselves. This means the neighbor next door and around the world. If the neighbor be among
the poor, the hungry, the oppressed and exploited, the under-
privileged of the earth, as is true of great numbers of the
world's population including many in our own land, the call to
helpfulness through economic, educational, legislative, or other
effective steps is imperative. This is why I have long been an
active exponent of the social gospel as a necessary aspect of our
total gospel.

Having stated my basic personal beliefs, I must turn now to
the matter of how they have affected, or perhaps have been
affected by, my personal living. This requires being somewhat
autobiographical. Let us begin with the church.

I was born and raised on a farm in a small rural community,
mainly Protestant, in northeastern New York. Until I was
sixteen I attended church and Sunday school in the local
schoolhouse—nothing then was heard in our community of the
separation of church and state. Beginning earlier than I can

remember, I regularly attended Sunday worship with my parents. It was as much a part of life's routine as going to meals. I have continued to attend church regularly ever since, and to participate in its activities. I have listened to all sorts of preaching, from the poorest to the best, but in all circumstances the church has continued to nourish my spirit. I have served often on local committees, six times as a delegate to the General Conference of my denomination (the United Methodist), and as a representative at several ecumenical world conferences. Thus I have seen the church in action at all levels, "warts and all," and I have never lost faith in it. I still believe that it is the primary and indispensable agent for the spread of the gospel and the advancement of God's kingly rule on earth.

As for my inner life, I believe greatly in the importance of prayer. Though my most recent book is entitled *Mysticism: Its Meaning and Message,* I am not a mystic as the term is usually understood. I have never found it essential to spend long periods of seclusion or silence in prayer, though I do pray daily and frequently and try to live in the light and the strength that God gives me. One of my most widely read books has been *Prayer and the Common Life,* and I believe that prayer ought to be part of the common life of every person. Were there more of it as a motivating and guiding force, our world today would be a better place.

As for critical periods in my life when its course was changed by prayer and what I believe to have been God's leading, I will mention some of them. As a sophomore in college, I attended a student picnic one evening at a dangerous place—on a cliff overhanging a gorge filled with water deep in some places and with surrounding rocks adjacent. I made a misstep and fell twenty-five feet, fortunately into the water and not on the rocks. But in the total darkness and not knowing how to swim, my chances of survival were slight. I prayed mightily, and God told me the one thing needful—to hold my breath while under the water and catch a quick breath each time I came to the surface. That and a brave rescue by a fellow student account for the fact that I have lived many years since that fateful evening.

In the early years of my teaching at Garrett, I had a difficult time. Between trying to keep up with my duties there and with the demands of the world as I accepted more invitations than was wise, I used up more energy than I had. At the same time, an apparently trivial spinal injury kept me in constant pain, and I "suffered much under many physicians." I suppose I came close to the edge of a nervous breakdown. But God delivered me through prayer, the wise counsel of my pastor, the love of friends, and the challenge of useful work to do within the limits of my strength.

Along life's way, there were the critical vocational adjustments to make. First, the decision in my student days to become a foreign missionary; then the decision not to because my parents needed me. As I sought a college teaching position, there were the rebuffs that came because a man was desired for the openings available. Then came the strategic invitation, unsought, that led to my teaching theology in a theological seminary, with much more fuss made over me than I deserved —perhaps more of a peril to the soul than the rebuffs had been! And later, the crucial decision to leave a large seminary where I was happy and probably somewhat useful, and come to a smaller one with a reduced schedule and more time for writing. In all these changes I feel that God was leading me, and I have no regrets.

I have greatly enjoyed the years of my retirement, and have kept comfortably busy in it. As I grow older, I am aware of the diminishing number of years before me. I do not think that I dread or fear death. When God has no further work for me to do, my hope is that he will let me pass peacefully from this earthly scene. But the times are in his hands.

So these are my thoughts on my personal beliefs and what I live by. Let the reader make of them what he will.

Rachel Henderlite

RACHEL HENDERLITE WAS BORN IN HENDERSON, North Carolina, in 1905. She received her B.A. from Agnes Scott College in Decatur, Georgia. She attended Biblical Seminary in New York City and earned her M.A. in Christian education from New York University. She holds a Ph.D. in Christian ethics from Yale Divinity School.

She was dean and professor of Bible at Mississippi Synodical College, Holly Springs, Mississippi, professor of Bible at Montreat College, Montreat, North Carolina, teacher of Bible at Harding High and Charlotte Technical School in Charlotte, North Carolina, and for sixteen years was professor of applied Christianity and Christian nurture at the Presbyterian School of Christian Education in Richmond, Virginia. She was director of educational research and director of curriculum development for the Board of Christian Education of the Presbyterian Church in the United States, before becoming professor of Christian education at the Austin Presbyterian Theological Seminary in Austin, Texas.

Her works include *Exploring the Old Testament, Exploring the New Testament, A Call to Faith, Paul: Christian and World Traveller, Forgiveness and Hope,* and *The Holy Spirit in Christian Education.* She was also instrumental in developing the Covenant Life Curriculum for her denomination. She was ordained to the gospel ministry in 1965.

Reflections of a P.K.

RACHEL HENDERLITE

As I REFLECT ON IT, MY WHOLE LIFE AND MY FAITH HAVE BEEN pressed and shaped by two divergent points of view, both of which are held within the Christian church. On the one hand, I was brought up in a typical congregation in the conservative Southern Presbyterian Church and spent my days in the so-called "Bible Belt." On the other hand, I early became a member of the church's larger academic community which was free to question and probe and for which no pattern of life, no structure of society was too sacred to criticize. What came out of this juxtaposition of viewpoints, I shall try to make clear.

As a teen-ager I was known as a P.K., and that designation probably offers the strongest single clue to the hold the Christian faith had upon me from my earliest days.

P.K., of course, means Preacher's Kid. At Montreat, North Carolina, our church's assembly grounds where we always went for summer vacation, there were three such titles—and the three together included all young people. M.K. meant Missionary's Kid. O.K. was Ordinary Kid and referred to all youngsters not blessed with either of the other titles. Being a P.K. or an M.K. carried disadvantages, of course, as well as advantages, and each had its own distinctive advantages and disadvantages. But I think unquestionably the two together connoted a distinct cultural pattern in those days, a way of life in which many of us were nurtured.

For me, being a P.K. was crucial. Perhaps I should say that being the daughter of this particular preacher was crucial. I

76

thought my dad was tops in every way. He, with my mother, shaped the home I grew up in. He shaped the theological beliefs that began to develop from my earliest years. From him we—my sister and brother and I—came to know the meaning of grace. We came ultimately to know our own worth, how to treat other people, what things were important and what were not. Over the years we absorbed his faith in God, his confidence in the integrity and understanding love of God which he held even though his own theological training had apparently included the doctrine of double predestination, which is so patently inconsistent with the doctrines of grace and redemption incarnated in Jesus Christ. He was still puzzling over these inconsistencies when I was finishing college and had long since abandoned them—and we had many intense conversations at the dinner table, in his study, and in the little Chevrolet he used for parish visiting. The most memorable part of the conversations was his stubborn refusal to surrender to textbooks if their pronouncements were alien to what he himself *knew* to be true.

I was a P.K. and I thank God for it.

Dad was a good preacher and a great pastor, and his congregation thrived on what he did and on what he had to say. Ours was a warm and friendly congregation. All of us knew everybody and we felt at home together. We had our vacation church schools and our church suppers as did other congregations in town. We had our full share of crooks and gossips and more than our share of rather insensitive owners and managers of textile mills. Dad was pastor for twenty-eight years in the town made famous, or infamous, by Liston Pope's *Millhands and Preachers.* He was pastor to a downtown church and active in community affairs. But nothing in his education for ministry had even raised the suspicion that he and these millowners he preached to had responsibility for the ultimate economic plight of the millhands. It was taken for granted that our responsibility for them was fulfilled in the little mission Sunday schools run by "Dr. Charlie," one of our elders, in one mill community after another.

Dad was far more sensitive to the plight of the Negro and had many friends and admirers among the "colored people" as they were called in the teens and twenties. As a child I used to go with him when he was invited to preach in a "colored" church. He was a member of an early interracial commission that worked to improve the schools the black children attended. But even in race relations there was little thought of questioning the *status quo.* The standards of society were not believed to be the business of the church. Our focus was on individuals within the system. The church I knew as a child was warm and comfortable and undisturbed by the injustices in the world around it.

But fortunately the church is larger than any one congregation. In due time I was sent to two church-related colleges and had the great experience of attending Y.W.C.A. and Y.M.C.A. conferences, where I heard Kirby Page, Stanley Jones, John R. Mott, Harry Emerson Fosdick, and many others who had the gift of flinging open windows and doors to questions that would never have had a chance in the congregation my father served—war and peace, industry and labor, Biblical criticism, racial equality.

One of my professors in college made a practice of inviting some of us into her apartment occasionally on Sunday evenings to meet and converse with individuals who were on the far edge of Christian and social thought. It was like a peepshow into a world of forbidden ideas. We were introduced to the ideas of free love, mercy killing, the emancipation of women.

The rest of my student life—and my father thought he would never get me educated—was characterized by this same alternation between what seemed the far left and what was surely the far right. Our church at home was a typical Southern Presbyterian Church. Many features of college life were just as conservative. But right in the middle of it, without any initiative on my part, a window would be flung open and startling new ideas would sweep in; or a world-famous leader would penetrate into my consciousness, shattering the protective covering of my unquestioning childhood.

Toward the end of my senior year I found myself laid flat with tuberculosis. That was before the wonder drugs had stopped that scourge, and so the disease stopped me. It seemed the end of the world to me then, but, on looking back after many years, I can see that it proved invaluable. For a year—and later on for two years—I had time for these two conflicting points of view to meet head on and find some measure of accommodation before I went on to graduate school and was subjected again to two widely different approaches to life and thought.

Both graduate schools were exciting, but in very different ways. The first was Biblical Seminary in New York City. Here the Bible was the field of study and here the Bible came alive for me. We spent little time on the critical apparatus of Bible study and we did not search for the original documents within the many redactions. But we did immerse ourselves in the English text of the Bible, letting the literary form in which we now have the Bible convey the Biblical message. The historical books became the *Heilsgeschichte* for us. The prophets shouted and prayed their way into our lives. The Gospels—why we almost knew them by heart! But, most of all, we knew what the church remembered of Jesus Christ and what the church thought he meant. I found myself wide-eyed at what God had done in human history. I had penetrated deeply into large portions of Scripture and I had been given a methodology for digging into other portions. My excitement drove me into teaching after my second bout with tuberculosis. I was eager to open this new world of Biblical thought to other people as it had been opened to me. I taught in camps and conferences. I taught Sunday school classes, women's circles, a business women's class that "really wanted to study." I taught in two junior colleges and two high schools. And I had the exhilaration of seeing other people captured by the same magnetism that had caught me up in my own study.

But, as time went on, my exhilaration wore thin. I was too much of a Calvinist to be comfortable when Bible study was separated from other disciplines. And so I began to look about for a graduate school where I could explore other branches of human thought. I finally settled on Yale, and in the fall of 1942, at the age of thirty-seven, I struck out for New Haven. Needless to say, I was scared. Who was I to go to an Ivy League school? Could I make it? Would I find there the richness of human wisdom I sought? One friend and colleague gave me a final warning as she reluctantly watched me leave home: "Well, it may be all right for you to go to Yale, but don't you let them change you!" I was hankering to be changed—hungering for something that had been left out of my experience.

I suppose I'll always bless the friends who called my attention to Yale Divinity School and encouraged me to go there. I'll always be grateful for the combination of circumstances that sent me there at the particular time, for it was a great time to be at Yale. Luther Allen Weigle was dean of the Divinity School. Kenneth Scott Latourette was head of the Department of Religion. I was steered by Dean Weigle into the field of Christian ethics and—blessed day!—put in the tutelage of H. Richard Niebuhr, who in turn enrolled me in multiple courses with Robert L. Calhoun and Liston Pope, the archenemy of my hometown and the relentless critic of my preacher-father. There were other "greats" at Yale also—Roland Bainton, Paul Vieth, Millar Burrows, Halford Luccock—but those three with whom I had most of my classes, Niebuhr, Calhoun, and Pope, were Yale for me. I had never known anything like their lectures. Manifesting ranges of thought and mastery of detail I had never dreamed of, they both destroyed me and re-created me. For the first six weeks I did not know what the words meant. They might as well have been speaking in a foreign language. Then things began to fall in place, and what I had taken with me to New Haven was restored and supported and enlarged.

No small contribution to my understanding of what was going on in my life was made by the dissertation I was led to write. Having in mind my interest in Christian education and my need for theological reflection, my professors steered me into a study of the theological basis of Horace Bushnell's *Chris-*

tian Nurture. The value of this study for me was in its valida-
tion of my experience as a child. A point of real conflict lay in
the juxtaposition of a Reformed understanding of church and
covenant with the essentially Baptist view of the church that
prevailed in the Bible Belt. I had been Bushnell's child who
grew up as a Christian and never knew himself/herself to be
other than Christian. Yet our congregation, like most congregations in town, held a series of revival services every fall which
were the occasion for the children of the congregation to "join
the church." I needed an opportunity to clarify and deal with
the issues at stake here. I needed to authenticate my own
experience of being enveloped in my father's faith and of
moving from that borrowed faith into a faith of my own that
could meet my expanding world. I found it in my study of
Bushnell and his conflict with nineteenth-century revivalism.

It was gratifying to me that, with all this expansion of ideas,
none of my father's faith which had enveloped my early years
had to go. The grace of God, his sovereignty, his transcendence
coupled with his immanence—these were not destroyed, although seriously challenged by the widely diversified reading I
did. On the contrary, they were enriched, filled full of meaning. I began to see these convictions of the church in some of
their complexity. I learned to make a place for ambiguity and
paradox. My association in large lecture classes and intimate
seminars, even in individual guided study, with men who it
seemed to me had read everything that was ever written and
yet were not afraid to say, "I haven't read that," was an experience to both humble and exalt a neophyte. I was inspired to
read hundreds of books I never knew existed, and I was enabled
to understand them, at least in part. Broad areas of Western
culture that had shaped my life willy-nilly were lifted to a level
where I could examine them. I came to understand what we
mean by the elusive term "the Christian faith" as I never had
before, although I had been nurtured in it. What is even more
important to me, since those student days I have never felt the
need to apologize for the Christian faith—although many
times for the Christian church.

Since then I have been teaching in various ways—in the classroom, in some books and articles I have written, in the curriculum for our denomination I have helped to develop. All these enterprises have made the same demand and offered the same opportunity, namely, that I clarify for other people, people of all shapes and sizes and from all sorts of backgrounds, what had become clear to me over some forty years of teaching and studying. The questions are: "What is God like?" and "What difference does it make?"

There is obviously no easy answer for such questions once you take into account the tragedy as well as the joy of human existence. A doctrine that seems to answer one question simply complicates another. And some situations raise questions for which there seems to be no verbal answer whatsoever. Over the years I developed one basic test for the answers I could give when these questions have been put to me in any of their many forms. Push back until you find the one conviction of which you are most confident, the one truth you are prepared to insist on. I won't say "the conviction you are ready to die for," because it may not be strong enough for that. Then ask yourself the questions: "If this is true, what else is likely to be true? What cannot be true? What are the implications of this conviction—for this and this and this area of your life?" You simply cannot hold as true any conclusions that are not consistent with the one truth you know to be true.

Such a formula will not get rid of all the questions that life (or some student) raises for you. But it does rescue you from the intolerable position of trying to hold two absolutely contradictory doctrines at the same time. And it does give you a starting point for developing a system of belief you can hold with integrity, albeit with some tentativeness.

For me this starting point has been the conviction that God can be understood best through Jesus Christ—in what Jesus said about God as the church remembered it, and in what the church believed Jesus himself was and did. Thus the word "Father" has been for me the most satisfactory word for talking about, or thinking about, God—a metaphor made apt by my own experience as a child.

As a child I had not always understood my own father. I had even doubted his love from time to time, and his fairness in dealing with his children. But never had I doubted his worth. It was rather my own worth that was called into question again and again. I suppose the greatest struggle human beings face in growing up is the struggle to reconcile love with judgment in the authority figure over us. At least this seems to be the case in my experience and that of many students who have come to me over the years. It is the struggle to secure a sense of one's own worth and at the same time to acknowledge the existence of a higher law that is binding on us and that we find impossible to obey. I had been teaching for years before this was settled for me in a way I could live with. Nevertheless, the outstanding fact of my childhood had been my father and, unlike a tragic number of human fathers, he served me well as a prototype for God.

As it finally shook down after years of struggle, my faith comes out looking something like this: God is like a father. Or, better, God *is* Father. He is the Father of all men, women, and children everywhere. He brought us all into being, placed each one of us into the stream of history at that point in time where we now find ourselves, to affect history as we can in response to God's own activities. He knows us. That is, he sees us clearly, with all our potential and all our limitations. He understands why we behave as we do. And he loves us, each one of us, with never-failing compassion, and even pride. Through this compassion and pride—which are the ingredients of grace—he frees us from all condemnation and ever holds open for us the possibility of new life. We do not have to be crippled by our past. We can always start again. Moreover, we can be agents through whom he will work to accomplish his ends in the world. God asks nothing of us but that we accept his love and consent to be part of his family. Whatever demand the Christian gospel carries follows out of the context of our understanding of God's intention for the world and of his claim upon us.

The word "adoption" has been crucial for me in grasping the significance of God's grace. I have known intimately for many years a family whose five children were adopted in babyhood one by one. They have had the most intriguing custom—possible, I suppose, only for an adoptive family—of celebrating for each member of the family not only a birthday but also the anniversary of the day that individual became a member of the family. The children have grown up knowing that the only ties they have to one another are ties of love and loyalty, as is true also in the family of God. They did not have to prove themselves before they were accepted as members. They simply come into the family and whatever "demand" there is comes later, as one becomes mature enough to love other members of the family more than one's self, and to understand and accept one's own and the family's role in the ongoing story of humankind.

But no need to go on and on. To any theologian who might be reading what I have to say, no doubt this is a gross oversimplification. It may even sound naïve to laymen. I am probably taking too little account of the complexities bound up in any theological system, and of the tragic circumstances of life that make unbelievable so simple a statement of faith. I am not tracing the schools of theology that have made my position tenable. I am merely setting forth what has indeed happened to one person who has been subjected to the influence of the church in a great variety of its expressions from early childhood to the moment of writing. It is an account of one who knew intimately the simple but questioning faith of a father, was wrapped up in it, and then was thrown with some of the great critical scholars of the church for an opportunity to explore the meaning of experiences that were already very real. This is, you might say, an account of a pilgrimage from being a Preacher's Kid to being the Church's Kid and the heir of the church's convictions and the church's questions.

E. Glenn Hinson

EDWARD GLENN HINSON IS A NATIVE OF ST. LOUIS,
Missouri, where he was born in 1931. He received his
B.A. from Washington University in St. Louis, his
B.D. and Th.D. from Southern Baptist Theological
Seminary in Louisville, Kentucky, and recently the
D.Phil. degree from Oxford University.

He has served as associate pastor of the First Baptist
Church in Affton, Missouri, and as pastor of the First
Baptist Church in Eminence, Indiana. Since 1959 he
has been a member of the faculty at Southern Baptist
Theological Seminary, Louisville, where he is cur-
rently professor of church history. He was named
"Professor of the Year" for 1968–1969.

His books include *The Church: Design for Survival;
Glossolalia,* a collaborative venture with Frank Stagg
and Wayne E. Oates; *Seekers After Mature Faith;* I
and II Timothy and Titus in The Broadman Bible
Commentary; and *A Serious Call to a Contemplative
Life-Style.* He has given the Southern Baptist Seminary Lectures at Carson-Newman College, Tennessee, and the Edwin Stephens Griffiths lectures at
South Wales Baptist College.

My Faith Is Paradoxical

E. GLENN HINSON

My faith is paradoxical. I have learned to accept that as a fact of Christian life. To present it intelligibly, I will have to explain it in terms of its paradoxes.

First, my faith is both highly individual and highly social. It is highly individual in the sense that it originates deep within the inner recesses of my personal being, my self. It represents a sovereign resolve, an act of will, a decision, a determination, or whatever else one may call it, to believe even though I cannot comprehend *(credo ut intelligam)*. It involves a decision about life's ultimate question that no other person can make for me. The question: Who am I in relation to all that is? Who else could answer that question for me? Not the scientist. Not the historian. Not the sociologist. Not the anthropologist. Not even the theologian. Even I cannot answer it as scientist, as historian, as sociologist, as anthropologist, as theologian. I answer it as a human being. And as a rational and perhaps suprarational being, I am compelled to give an answer.

Yet, at the same time, my faith is highly social. I have reached this decision because a lot of people led me toward the point of decision. I do not know what the input of each one may have been, but each person whom I have met, both within and outside the church, may have helped to form the corridor that led me to this threshold. Some persons have affected me profoundly. My mother—a person of mystical temperament who belonged simultaneously to a Baptist church and to a Spiritualist church. My father—who professed now atheism

and now theism as he wallowed through the mire of alcohol-
ism. My older brother—who pondered with me in serious
moments the realities of life and death. A grandmother—who
shared the example of staunch and unflinching Baptist piety in
the face of poverty, long widowhood, and disappointments. A
saintly aunt and uncle—who did not scold or chide but who
gently encouraged church involvement by their faithfulness. A
pastor—who helped to guide growth in discipleship by parcel-
ing out jobs just one hand's length ahead of where I was at a
certain time. Professors at college (Washington University, St.
Louis)—who dunned me again and again with the query,
"How do you know?" and would not let me rest content with
a self-serving vocation but kept asking, "What real contribution will you make to the life of mankind through your career?"
I could go on.

Second, as you may detect already, my faith is both simple
and complex. It is simple in that it boils down to belief that
God is as personal being, as the heavenly Father, and that I will
trust him no matter what. This is a naïve conclusion, I know.
But I learned through much agony of spirit what many others
have also learned. You cannot prove God. You cannot demon-
strate his existence. To be sure, you can cite the classical
arguments for God's existence—the Unmoved Mover, the Un-
caused Cause, the Great Designer, the sense of moral ought-
ness, the ontological argument, and all the rest. And these will
be helpful to the person who is predisposed already to believe.
But the person who is not predisposed to believe will be able
to match every argument with a counterargument that is
equally convincing to him—so, at least, I found in college when
I tried to prove that God, however we describe him, exists. My
experience convinces me that Blaise Pascal, the brilliant seven-
teenth-century French mathematician and philosopher, was
right. In the end, it comes down to a gamble that God is. In
this case, it is necessary to gamble because we are dealing with
the ultimate question of life. And it is better to wager that God
is than that he is not. For if I wager that he is and it turns out
that he is not, then I have lost nothing. But if I wager that he

is not and it turns out that he is, then I have lost everything. So my faith is very simple. It is a simple belief that God is as the heavenly Father who takes care of his own. He is, again as Pascal said in his famous *Memorial,* not the God of the philosophers and the learned, but the Father of Abraham, Isaac, Jacob, the Father of Jesus Christ—your God and my God. He is found, not by rational investigation or debate, but by the ways taught in the gospel.

Yet, at the same time, my faith is complex. I have an inquiring mind which seeks understanding. By virtue of this desire to know and in the light of my religious experience, my faith totters on the brink between doubt and conviction. It says, "Lord, I believe; help thou mine unbelief" (Mark 9:24). I do not mean by this that I am lying awake nights reexamining the fundamental conviction to which I came years ago. I resolved that issue in college days when I found I could not answer the skeptic's demand to "prove" everything by empirical or logical argument. I had lain awake many nights trying to figure out the ultimate "proofs" for God's existence. One night as I drifted off in a kind of semiconscious stupor, this issue searing my mind, I jerked awake and sat bolt upright in bed. John 8:32 was burning in my mind: "And ye shall know the truth, and the truth shall make you free." At the time I could not have done a satisfactory exegesis of the text, but the conclusion that followed set me free. If God, if Christ, is truth, I reasoned, then nothing I discover by any other method of investigation will conflict with that truth. This was an anchor, firmly snagged, to which I could tie a line and let my boat drift in any direction to seek truth in its partial and fragmentary forms. If new discoveries rang true in empirical observation or to reason, I could accept them. They would not overturn this answer to life's ultimate question, Who am I in relation to all that is?

I have never departed from this conviction. But it has freed me to be a seeker of truth; indeed, it has made me a seeker of truth. And my stock answer to those who not infrequently warn, "But aren't you jeopardizing your career by saying or teaching that?" is: "I am conscience-bound to one thing, the truth." However much the pursuit of truth costs, I could wish I might always be willing to pay. No one, of course, can forecast what he may do when the chips are down, but principle should always take precedence over expediency.

My fundamental conviction that God is as personal being produces a third paradox for my faith, both an intense concern and an equivalent lack of concern about answering every religious question that people ask. This will be evident as I list some specific points in my theology.

First, about God. I blow my mind trying to frame a concept of God that is large enough to correspond to a scientific understanding of the universe. God has to be big enough to engage in a continuous creative process over billions and billions of years and involving a universe that pulsates in space through millions of light-years. He has to be big enough to direct the whole universe toward some purposeful end while allowing various aspects of it, especially man, enough freedom to work for or against that end. He has to be free himself from this creation and yet so involved in it as to suffer when it does not fulfill his purposes for it.

All our human analogies fail us in trying to describe God and his activity. But I like to use the analogy of love. "God is love" (I John 4:8). Love creates. Love both pours itself into what it creates and remains greater than it is. Love suffers with what it creates. So we may think of the motive force within the universe as this love, God himself. His love, to quote the popular song, "makes the world go round." It directs the world toward some ultimate purpose. And here and there it surfaces in a particular way in the creation and especially in human history to tell us where it is directing us. It has probably surfaced in universal human experience, in the experience of other religions, but it has surfaced in a special way in Israel's religion and in Jesus of Nazareth. In the latter, God has shown that he is on our side, ranging himself with us and for us. He has told us that life, despite all evidences to the contrary, does have some meaning and purpose, that it is not moving at random.

Second, about man. Basically, I am an optimistic realist.

Whether by observation or by reading the Scriptures, I know that man is capable of both good and evil. Evil is not a consequence of any inherent defect of nature; it is a perversion of what is good, for the whole creation is inherently good. God has created man in such a way that man is capable of accepting responsibility for his own life. God does not violate this freedom. Instead, he intervenes in man's life to the extent that man invites him to intervene. He relates to the creation, particularly to man, like the chess master rather than like the great clockmaker. This means that you and I may have several choices, any one of which could be God's will for our lives in the sense that he may use these to fulfill his ultimate purpose. In other words, I don't believe that everything is either/or. In retrospect, I can be perfectly convinced that a particular thing was God's will. In looking forward, however, I often have to choose between a large number of possible alternatives. Should I teach? Should I be a pastor? Should I work in a grocery? Should I sell shoes? God, then, is powerful enough to take whatever choice I make and to fit it into a larger scheme of things. Is this not what Paul means when he says, "God works all things together for good for those who love him, for those who are called according to his purpose"? (Rom. 8:28.)

Third, about life. It is this conviction regarding freedom which lies behind my optimistic realism. On the one hand, I am well aware that things do not always turn out right in the moment. Life can be shattering. Illness, joblessness, death, failure, rejection, defeat—a whole range of large and small crises can cause anxiety. Under such circumstances faith is tested. How one weathers severe storms in life depends upon a conviction that life has some larger purpose and that even those things can lead to something more hopeful. Indeed, whether one can find any meaning in the midst of the tediums of life depends upon the same conviction. I like the answer Teilhard de Chardin, Jesuit philosopher and paleontologist, once gave a friend of his engaged in business who had asked about the value of his immersion in his business. "Because you are doing the best you can (even though you may sometimes fail)," he wrote, "you are forming your own self within the world, and you are helping the world to form itself around you. How, then, could you fail from time to time to feel overcome by the boundless joy of creation?" (*Letters from a Traveller*, p. 120; London: Collins, 1962). This is not just fatalism, a shrugging of shoulders, "What will be will be." Is it not, rather, the exercise of faith which Jesus demanded when he used the lilies, the sparrows, and the hairs of our head as object lessons? (Matt. 6:25–33.) As a believer, I do what I can and leave the rest to the heavenly Father. I need not be anxious and fretful, for I know that he cares as much, perhaps more, than I, even though he does not violate the freedom which he has assured us.

Existentially here is where the water hits the wheel for me as a Christian. At the age of twenty-eight I began to lose my hearing partially. On the heels of this, while burning the candle at both ends in order to finish my doctoral dissertation and to teach at the same time, I began to lose my voice. The loss of one faculty is a crushing blow, the loss of two devastating. I became nervous, fretful. What would be my future as a teacher? How could this happen to me? The skyrocketing of anxiety multiplied the speaking difficulties. It pushed me lower and lower. Finally, I rediscovered what I had learned before but what I had also forgotten—that every man has one recourse in a situation that he cannot surmount by the sheer force of his will. He has to trust God, other people, himself. My voice has been recovered with but a slight chronic laryngitis. I will not recover my hearing. But I can live with both. And the experience has added immeasurably to what I am as a person. It has schooled me for meeting life without the anxiety that is so characteristic of every age of man.

Fourth, about communion with God. How is faith nourished and strengthened in order to meet the exigencies of life? For me the answer is communion with God. This has not meant a succession of exhilarating mountaintop experiences. Rather, my experience has been more like that of the Children of Israel, often in the desert and seldom on the mountain. But I have learned to exercise discipline in devotion, not as a rigid semimonastic routine of prayer and church attendance but as fitted to my own schedule and personality.

One thing I have had to get settled is the real reason for prayer or for other acts of devotion. For a long time I prayed selfishly, for what I could get out of it, as most of us do. The trouble with that is, I found less and less reason to pray because modern scientific expertise increasingly offers solutions to emotional, physical, and even spiritual problems. So, for a time, I said: "Why pray at all? I will express my devotion to God in my activities." The trouble with this attitude, I found, was that all activities soon leveled off to a single plane. I came to the conclusion then that we should pray because we believe that God is as the heavenly Father. We are personal beings. Therefore we desire to commune with him as personal being. Our love responds to him as Love.

Given the view of God which I discussed earlier, our communion with him may take several forms. It may involve a turning on to the presence of God within his handiwork, nature. Or, because the modern metropolis makes it difficult for many to have contact with nature, it may involve turning on to his presence in the face of our brother. Our communion may occur also through turning inward in meditation. Hundreds of college youths today are taking courses in transcendental meditation taught by the Maharishi Mahesh Yogi. Psychologists and psychiatrists are trying to teach their patients how to meditate. So far as I can see, these methods do not differ from Christian meditation. But our presuppositions do differ. In our journey inward we expect to find our selves in the Self, that is, in God. I find it helpful to remember the belief of the medieval mystics that God is he whose center is everywhere, whose circumference is nowhere. This means that his center of consciousness is in me. What I have to do in order to experience his presence is to open my inner self to him. Our communion may occur also by turning over our lives to God for the fulfillment of his purposes. To me this is the most truly Christian prayer that we may utter. It is the prayer of surrender, putting myself at God's disposal.

Communion with God also involves communion with other believers, i.e., the church. I believe in the church, even in its institutional form. To be sure, it has faults. It has often failed to fulfill God's purpose for it. It seldom displays his love as it should. It sometimes obstructs his purpose. Nevertheless, my communion with God draws me into communion with other Christians. As an ordained minister, I confess that I sometimes struggle to avoid being a churchman only in a professional way —speaking, teaching, praying when asked. I have tried to avert this by not filling my calendar with appointments which would keep me professionally engaged all the time. I attend church when I am not engaged. And I still thrill to see faithful laymen who attend every meeting simply because they love Christ and his church.

Finally, about death and beyond. To a large degree, I have to leave matters of death, life after death, and heaven and hell in God's hands. I cannot honestly say, either by study of the Scriptures or by other means, what happens at death. I am confident that no good thing which I have done during my life will have been a total loss. Because I believe that God is personal, I am inclined also to believe that he conserves us as persons. That is, we go on sharing in his personal existence. As he is, so we are. Love continues to sustain us.

My views of heaven and hell would have to mesh with this understanding. Obviously, accepting the modern scientific view of the universe as I do, I cannot conceive of either in spatial terms—heaven "up there" and hell "down there." For me, heaven implies participation in God's love, hell deprivation of it. In his earthly "threescore and ten," therefore, man already experiences these. They play opposite roles in his formation as a person, and his formation as a person will continue beyond this present life. Some persons, by their own resolve closing their heart's door to God, never reach full personhood. They wither and die, consumed as it were by their separation from the source of life. Others, insofar as possible letting the divine light within kindle their love, keep on growing until God becomes all in all.

This leaves a lot of oft-asked questions unanswered. But I prefer to close my statement that way. By its very nature, faith leaves something unspoken. It is but "the substance of things hoped for, the evidence of things not seen" (Heb. 11:1). It leaves a nimbus around life. What I have done has been to cast my anchor where you can see how my life is moored. Held by that anchorage, I will continue to ask, seek, knock, trusting God to take care of things that I cannot comprehend.

Archibald M. Hunter

Archibald M. Hunter was born in Kilwinning, Ayrshire, Scotland, in 1906. He holds the M.A., B.D., Ph.D. degrees and the honorary D.D. degree from the University of Glasgow, and the D.Phil. degree from Oxford. He has also studied in Marburg.

For six years he was pastor of the Church of Scotland in Perthshire, and for six years was professor of New Testament at Mansfield College, Oxford. From 1945 until his retirement in 1971, he was professor of New Testament at Aberdeen University, and for twelve of those years also master of Christ's College, the divinity school of the Church of Scotland.

He has been much in demand as a lecturer on both sides of the Atlantic, giving the Sprunt Lectures at Union Theological Seminary in Richmond, Virginia. Among his more than twenty books are a number that have been widely used by ministers and laymen. His best-known works include *Introducing the New Testament, The Work and Words of Jesus, The Gospel According to St. Paul,* and *A Pattern for Life.*

Why I Am a Christian

ARCHIBALD M. HUNTER

"WHEN A MAN ASKS YOU WHY YOU ARE A CHRISTIAN," SAYS Peter, "always be ready to give him an intelligent answer." (See I Peter 3:15.)

That was nineteen hundred years ago, when the wicked Roman emperor Nero began to persecute the Christians. Today, no less than in Nero's day, when the Christian faith is again on trial in the world, the same readiness is being demanded of us. In many lands, even our own, the Christian church, Christian doctrine, and Christian morality are being openly challenged and not seldom repudiated. If, then, we mean to be real Christians and not merely nominal ones, we ought to be able and ready to give a reason for the faith that is in us.

Why are you a Christian? Suppose a Communist suddenly fired that question at you, how would you answer? Well, no doubt different Christians would give different answers, but at the end of the day the answers would boil down to one or two fundamentals. If that question were put to me, there are three things I would want to say, and maybe, if I explain them, they will suggest the basis for an answer.

First, then, I am a Christian *because Christianity offers me a Lord and Master whom any man might be proud to serve.* For me,

Christ is "the Lord of all good life." What do I mean by this?

Ever since man became conscious of the difference between right and wrong, he has pondered the question, What is the good life? It is because Christ's answer commends itself to me as the best that I call him "the Lord of all good life."

Better than any other he teaches me how to live: how to treat my family, my neighbors, my friends, my enemies. He makes love the master key of morals. He sums up the whole duty of man to his fellowman in the Golden Rule: Always treat others as you would like them to treat you. He teaches that true greatness lies in readiness to serve. He summons to selfless and sacrificial living and himself goes to the cross to redeem men from their sin.

And all through his own life I find goodness, courage, gentleness, and truth such as I find in no other. In short, when I look at that life and study that teaching, I cannot doubt that that is how God meant men to live.

But Christ gives me more than pattern; he gives me also power. He not only shows me what the good life is; he helps me with the living of it. Day by day, committing myself afresh to him, I find by experience that I am enabled to lead a better life; and though I may never be able to say with Paul, "I can do all things in him who strengthens me" (Phil. 4:13), I know very well that without his help I should be a very much worse man than I am.

Here then is a divine pattern for living, and a Lord to help with the living of it, that need not fear comparison with any other in all the world.

Next, I am a Christian *because Christianity makes sense for me of the riddle of existence.*

Why are we here at all? What is the meaning of life? Is there a purpose in our human joys and sorrows? And to what dark and mysterious shore are we steering?

These are the great ultimate questions—old, but ever new —with which every man who takes life seriously must make his reckoning. It is because Christianity gives me the only satisfying answer to them that I am a Christian. But what is the Christian answer?

Behind this mysterious universe there is not a blind and inscrutable Fate but a gracious heavenly Father. He made us; and, when we had fallen from grace, in Christ his Son he rescued us from our sins. His whole purpose in thus making and redeeming us was to create a great family of sons and daughters living forever in fellowship with him, and trained for this high destiny by the disciplines of earth.

What does this mean? It means that our life here is a kind of education that the almighty Father puts us through. Here on earth, by joy and by sorrow, by happiness and by suffering, we are being disciplined and trained that we may be fit persons to enjoy all those blessed things that God has prepared for those who love him.

This—or something very like it—is the Christian answer. And I say to you—not without knowledge of the other answers —that it is far and away the noblest and the best. On this view, your life, my life, take on a new dignity. We are no longer merely cattle of a superior breed who have our little day and die. We are spiritual beings, given, in Christ, the chance of becoming the sons of God; and this world, though terribly marred by human sin and wickedness, is still a bit of our Father's property, a room in his vast house, a training ground for life eternal. This is the Christian answer, and, accepting it, you can say:

> This is my Father's world;
>   O let me ne'er forget
> That though the wrong seems oft so strong,
>   God is the Ruler yet.

Finally, I am a Christian *because Christianity offers me the blessed hope of everlasting life.*

In other words, in the Christian hopes and promises I find the best grounds for believing that death is not an end but a beginning: not a terminus but a milestone on an everlasting road.

To be sure, I may find support for belief in an afterlife elsewhere: in the ineradicable human instinct that the dead live on, in the high arguments of philosophers from Plato to Kant, perhaps even in some of the better evidence provided by the Spiritualists. But, when I am asked to give a reason for the hope that is in me, it is upon two strong pillars in the Christian temple of truth that I rest my confidence.

The first is the *character of God* as he has revealed himself in Christ. If God is such a Father as Christ declared him to be, loving us with an invincible love and prepared to sacrifice his only Son to save us, he cannot allow "the last enemy," death, to break forever the strong bands that bind us to himself. Are we to believe that the purposes of the all-wise Father will be defeated by a germ, by a fall of coal, by a drunken taxi driver, by a surgeon's mistake? No, when God loves *once,* he loves *forever.* Death for the Christian is not a passing to extinction—not a candle blown out never to be relighted—but, as it was for Christ, a going to be with the Father.

The second strong pillar is the resurrection of Christ himself. With a full knowledge of the evidence for that stupendous event I cannot doubt that the men of the New Testament are right—that Christ conquered death and showed himself alive to many witnesses. I am convinced that he is living now. I remember his words, "Because I live, you will live also" (John 14:19). And I take to myself his promise and wait for the day when it will come true. On these two pillars—the strong love of God and the fact of a living Christ—I rest my hope.

We started from the need to give the inquirer reasons for the faith that was in us. I haven't exhausted the answers, but have I given you a basis for answers of your own?

Can you say with me, "I am a Christian because Christianity gives me a Lord and Master whom any man might be proud to serve, because Christianity makes sense for me of the riddle of existence, and because it offers me the blessed hope that death, so far from being the ending of the road, is but the doorway to a Father's house on high"?

> That creed I fain would keep,
>   That hope I'll not forgo,
> Eternal be my sleep—
>   Unless to waken so.

James Kallas

JAMES KALLAS, JR., WAS BORN IN CHICAGO, ILLINOIS, in 1928. He did his undergraduate work at St. Olaf College and earned his B.Th. degree at Luther Seminary in St. Paul, Minnesota. His M.A. is from Alliance Française, Paris, and his Ph.D. from the University of Southern California. He has also studied at the University of Durham, England, and the Goethe Institut in Munich, Germany. He has received Phi Beta Kappa, Fulbright, and Rockefeller Scholarships.

He was a college honor athlete, winning twelve letters in three sports, and later was a professional football player. Upon his ordination, he was called to the French Cameroon as director of Protestant mission schools under the aegis of the Board of World Missions of the American Lutheran Church. Later he became professor of religion at the California Lutheran College, a position he still holds. He is much in demand as a lecturer on college and university campuses. He is a member of the Board of World Missions of The American Lutheran Church.

Selected titles from his list of books include *The Significance of the Synoptic Miracles, The Satanward View: A Study in Pauline Theology, Jesus and the Power of Satan, The Story of Paul,* and *A Layman's Introduction to Christian Thought.*

God
Will Have the Last Word

JAMES KALLAS

MY FATHER WAS A PART OF THAT WAVE OF IMMIGRANTS RIGHT after World War I who, disillusioned and discouraged by the turmoils of the old country, came to America with the deliberate intention of making a clean break, a total break, with the old way of life.

That feeling, that attitude toward that which he left, had all kinds of implications for the religious life of my early years. I was born in Chicago, 1928, the eve of the Depression, and was baptized into the Greek Orthodox Church (my father had come from Greece, the Pelopponesian peninsula, south of Corinth, near Sparta)—and that baptism was the full and total extent of my adolescent exposure to religion! Determined deliberately to set aside ties to the Old World, dominated by the grinding poverty of Depression days, disenchanted by the lack of vigor apparent in the American branch of the Greek Orthodox Church of forty years ago, my father felt that the religious necessities of rearing his children were all discharged with the act of baptism. And so I grew up, on the lower west side of the city of Chicago, not antireligious but oblivious to religion, outside its pale, unaffected, unconcerned, and disinterested. And that's the way it went, right on through my high school days.

My last year in high school was a turning point. I didn't see it as such then—it is only retrospect that shows it to be a time of turning, a forging of a new direction. I played halfback on our high school football team, the leading scorer, a "star" in the exalted language of teen-age enthusiasm. And so, in that senior high school year, I was offered a football scholarship to the University of Nevada, in Reno. I was all set to go there when, at the last minute, my high school football coach asked me—before I made my final decision—if I would like to visit his alma mater, a small school in Minnesota, St. Olaf College. He would pay the way up, train ticket, expenses, if I just went and looked at his old school.

Had I gone on to school in Reno, I would probably still be in Nevada, with a little green lampshade over my eyes dealing blackjack in some casino! But back in those days I never turned down anything that was free, so, before saying "yes" to Reno and the University of Nevada, I accepted the train trip up to Northfield, Minnesota.

It was a beautiful spring day when I got there, and only those who have seen St. Olaf in the springtime know how stirringly beautiful it can be! As I went up the hill of St. Olaf Avenue, there was a magnificent limestone building, the Administration Hall, on my left, another magnificent limestone building, the library, on my right, and between those two about one hundred yards of sparkling green grass, every square foot of which was covered by young men lying flat on their backs, their books under their heads, whistling at the pretty blond Scandinavian girls walking by. I decided right then and there, "This is where I am going to spend the next four years!"

I didn't know, when I put down my $50 room deposit, that St. Olaf was a college of the Lutheran Church. I didn't find that out until later, and when I did find it out it was too late to get my money back. So I had to go! That was my introduction to the church.

I went into St. Olaf indifferent to religion—and came out hostile to it! My first formal introduction to the Christian religion left scars all over me. I was assigned a part-time job drying dishes in the college cafeteria. Just about all the students there were not only Scandinavians—they were Christians; at least they came from Christian homes. I was a rarity, the exciting exception, the black sheep, Greek, non-Christian, fair

game, fine target for the evangelistic energies of my dish-drying
companions. They descended on me! I felt like a lonely pioneer
on the plains of wild Indian country, pursued by those who
would take my scalp, trying to win me over to Jesus so I could
be one more star in their spiritual crown. With much mis-
directed zeal they tried to win me to the Lord. I was evangel-
ized, sermonized, and propagandized. Bible verses were hurled
at my head, hellfire was held to my feet. I was argued with,
pleaded with, denounced, exhorted.

I got scared. I went from bewilderment to amusement and
back to bewilderment—before I turned to cynicism. Cynicism
because all of us at that age lacked theological depth, and the
only Christianity they were trying to unload on me, from what
I could see, was a series of negative restrictions. Don't drink,
don't smoke or dance, don't play cards, and don't date any girls
who drink, dance, smoke, or play cards and you are a Christian.
Cynicism because two of the most ardent advocates of that
Christian posture, a young boy and a young girl, the most
energetic of the evangelists working on me, were suspended
from school after six weeks because they were caught in bed
together.

I didn't think I needed *any* kind of religion, but I was sure
that if I did need one, it certainly wasn't *that* kind of negative,
hypocritical posturing which preached one thing and practiced
another! So I became cynical, and, remembering an axiom of
the football field, "The best defense is a good offense," I went
from defending myself against their evangelistic forays over to
attacking the religious principles on which the school was
founded.

I suppose staid and conservative old St. Olaf College had
never had—and hasn't had since—a moment quite like that!
Yes, I am sure they had agnostics, and their share of armchair
Christians and sunshine soldiers, students out of church homes
who really didn't endorse the Christian convictions of those
church homes. But never had St. Olaf had an outright attacker,
one who would ardently and occasionally even eloquently try
to expose the intellectual inadequacies of the faith, holding its

practices up to ridicule and blasphemous scoffing. (I've been told, I don't know if it is true or not, that when I enrolled later at Luther Seminary to study for the ministry, one of the seminary professors who had read some of my student diatribes actually resigned from the seminary faculty!) From indifferent to bewildered to hostile. That was my religious biography the first twenty years of my life.

But while I was at St. Olaf, two things happened. One, even as I was attacking Christianity, I was being taught to think like a Christian. I didn't know that at the time, of course, but it was happening. Education is more than the accumulation of data and dates, it is more than an intellectual cafeteria through which one wanders selecting a course in calculus here, English literature there, topping it all off with basketweaving or Spanish grammar. To be educated is not simply to memorize the date of Frederick Barbarossa's death or to be able to plot the course of Hannibal across the Alps. Those bits of information might help you win a washing machine on a quiz program, but they don't make you an educated person! Education is more than all that, more than a summary of the facts that you learn. Education is the formation of a perspective, the building up of a frame of reference, the development of a point of view, the establishment of a base on which you stand and from which you make all your decisions. True education takes all the mass of material and synthesizes it into one whole, a whole that stands behind every decision you make later on in life. And during those college years, even though I didn't know it then, I was being taught to think like a Christian, to evaluate every problem of academic life from the standpoint of the church. I was being propagandized, brainwashed, intellectually formed without even being aware of it!

In an English class, I was not only reading Dostoevsky but being given a Christian interpretation of life through Dostoevsky! In *Crime and Punishment* young Raskolnikov comes back from student life in Europe infected by the "God is dead" philosophy of Nietzsche. The first thing he does is to murder an old lady with an ax. He had learned his lessons well! Nietzsche had said that God was dead, there was no ear in the heavens to hear our plea. But Nietzsche was deeper than that, more ruthlessly consistent than that. He argued that if there was no God, there was no brotherhood either. If God was not my father, my neighbor was not my brother! And so out of his denial of God, there grew his dog-eat-dog superman philosophy, the weak to the wall, the strong have no obligation to the weak. Spill out someone else's bucket of happiness if it will increase your own by a single drop. Raskolnikov had learned that lesson well and he murdered the old pawnbroker lady with an ax, spilling out her blood to increase his own happiness with her money.

But when he came back from Europe to Russia, he had returned to the bosom of the church. In those days, pre-Bolshevik Russia was a Christian nation, and, in the eyes of Slavophiles like Dostoevsky, Russia was seen as messiah, as mother Russia redeeming the world with its Christian faith, standing as a rock against the nihilistic anarchy of Europe and Nietzsche. As the story unfolds, Raskolnikov eventually turns himself in, confesses his crime, and asks for punishment. He does that at exactly the same moment that the one person who could have turned him in is committing suicide! Irony? Coincidence? Sarcasm by Dostoevsky? Is he sardonically trying to suggest that if Raskolnikov would only have waited, he would have finally been free, because the only person who could betray his crime was gone? Not at all! Dostoevsky was saying that the young man was being redeemed, was becoming a human being again. He had come back to mother Russia, the church, he had returned to the bosom of Christianity, he was being expurgated, cleansed from the diabolical traces of nihilism! He was once more becoming moral! He was able to see that he had done wrong and thus must be punished. . . . Crime and Punishment. The church had cleansed him.

That is the way I was being taught to think. I could multiply the examples endlessly, going into every academic department. In science, we were taught not only theorems and equations and tables of elements but also that behind the ordered chemical equations there was the hand of a loving, concerned God who was not capricious but who did all things well. Even as he made an intricate crystalline formation out of a single fleck of coal dust which today is and tomorrow is cast into the fire, so every human being is a unique and unparalleled divine accomplishment. In philosophy, we studied the same great minds as in a secular school: Bacon, Spinoza, Kant, and Mills. But whereas we studied the same men, we asked different questions or saw different answers. We were told that although men could ask the question "What is man?" only God could answer it, only the Scripture could give a final answer. Plato could say that man was good, self-determining and free, always walking down the avenue of the greatest good. But then we were told that the true image of man was seen in the cross of Jesus. That man was not so good. Confronted by kindness and mercy and loving concern, "good" man had cried out, "Crucify him!" But that was not the final word on the nature of man. Even as we spread his arms in hate to crucify him, he spread those arms even farther and breathed a benediction, "Father, forgive them; for they know not what they do." That is the final answer to the question "What is man?" He is a sinner. But a sinner loved of God, loved even unto death. The measure of a man, his ineffable grandeur and merit, his unquenchable dignity, is not that he can land rockets on the moon or conquer cancer or launch urban renewal programs. His merit is found in the fact that despite his sin he is loved of God.

That is what was taking place in me, even though I didn't know it. I was being given a vision, a staggering, earthshaking vision of stupendous scope. I was being told that even though I was kicking and struggling, writing defamatory articles against the church, ridiculing and scoffing, God loved me nonetheless.

The second thing that happened to me is really the first thing that happened to me—a thing of such immeasurable human importance that all else seems pale and shadowy in comparison. A young girl fell in love with me. And I with her. In my senior year we sat on a little hilltop behind Old Main,

Northfield away in the mists of the horizon. And we talked.
The whole world was wrapped in sparkling cellophane, a day
never to be forgotten. I began with talk of a baseball game, but
her blond hair was soaked with sun and baseball seemed so
unimportant then. We held hands and then we kissed. It was
not the first time. And yet it was the beginning of a new life.
She loved me, and I loved her, and each year since has seemed
to get richer. She was the joy of my life, the comfort in my pain,
that heart of me more important than my own. Darlean was,
and is, a Christian. And slowly under her delicate and tender
hand, the chip on my shoulder was taken away, my hostility to
the church was dissolved in her love toward Jesus, large enough
then for both of us.

We got married. I was graduated. I went on to play professional football with the old Chicago Cardinals (now the St.
Louis Cardinals). I didn't play long. I broke my shoulder, and
was cut from the roster the same day. I was a good college
player and would have been a good professional one too. But
there were lots of good college and professional players, and
when that shoulder cracked, my dreams and aspirations crum-
bled with it. The day I was cut from the squad, my arm in a
sling, I stood on the railway platform of Beaver Dam, Wiscon-
sin, site of the Cardinal training camp. The moment is en-
graved indelibly in my mind; I will carry it to the grave. I had
been a vigorous athlete, conference champion in the 100- and
220-yard dashes, college record holder in both, leading home
run hitter on the baseball team, had attained academic honors
as well (Phi Beta Kappa), and was editor of the college year-
book. But most of all, I was a football player, first-string halfback for four college years, signed to play professionally. And
now at the railway station the long shining steel rails fading in
the distance danced through the tears in my eyes. I was no
longer a football player. At age twenty-one my world had
ended.

But Darlean was there, she held the hand not in a sling. We
waited hours for that train to come, and in the quiet of my
despair came a counsel of Christian conviction, the assurance

that had strengthened so many others down the corridor of centuries. At the railway station I was told that God loved me, that broken bones and broken hopes are tomorrow's promise of healing, that in the church year Good Friday was always followed by Easter, that out of despair there came new life, new beginnings, and all was yet in front of us.

Under her gentle persuading I went to the seminary a year later, at first with doubts, later with faith, finally with enthusiastic conviction. Like Jacob of old, that which I had once fought against I now embraced. Like Paul of old, that which I once persecuted I preached. The power of God, able to pick up a man, turn him inside out, set him off in new directions, inject purpose and power and dignity into what was earlier aimless and angry, that same power is yet active.

Why am I in the church? Because consecrated faculty people at St. Olaf, in the face of the railing of a frightened youngster, continued serenely assured of what they believed, and shared it with me? Yes. Because a pretty young girl, her hair soaked in sunlight, loved me and led me? Yes. But most of all because behind them both stands a reality called the resurrection, which has claimed me as its own. A resurrection which tells us there is no room for doubt or despair because God will have the last word. A resurrection which tells us that hovering over us, concerned and omnipotent, loving and everlasting, is a God of power and love who conquers death and thus makes life rich and full, promising and victorious.

Gerald Kennedy

GERALD KENNEDY WAS BORN IN BENZONIA, MICHIgan, in 1907. He earned his A.M. and B.D. degrees from the Pacific School of Religion, and his S.T.M. and Ph.D. degrees from The Hartford Seminary Foundation.

He has held pastorates in Collinsville, Connecticut; San Jose, California; Palo Alto, California; Lincoln, Nebraska; and Pasadena, California. He was elected Bishop in the Methodist Church at the age of forty, the youngest man ever to hold that office. He served in the Portland, Oregon, and the Los Angeles areas until his retirement from the episcopacy in 1972. He has served as lecturer and visiting professor at various times in the Pacific School of Religion, Nebraska Wesleyan University, the School of Theology at Claremont, and Fuller Theological Seminary in Pasadena. He gave the Lyman Beecher Lectures at Yale in 1954.

In addition to the many offices he has held in the Methodist Church, he has been a member of the General Board of the National Council of Churches, Director of Goodwill Industries of Southern California, and a member of the California Board of Education. His books number twenty-five, including *For Preachers and Other Sinners, For Laymen and Other Martyrs,* and *The Preacher and the New English Bible.*

111

Jesus Was Right

GERALD KENNEDY

MOST OF THE THEOLOGIANS I HAVE READ SEEM TO ME TO BE a special group using a special kind of speech to explain their positions and their problems. It always makes me feel ill at ease to be labeled a "theologian." I would feel much more at ease if it were simply a matter of describing my faith and my doubts as a preacher of our time.

I shall, therefore, simply use this brief word as a means of stating my beliefs about the Christian faith, my assurances, and some of my doubts. I am in no sense a "professional" theologian. I am really a rather simple Christian telling some other Christians what I have found to be deep and eternal in the Christian faith.

I have a deep respect for theologians, and a great humility in trying to take my place in their fellowship. There have been times when I have tried to wrestle with theological problems, but always I have a strong feeling that I am too simple a Christian to be numbered among those theologians.

There are some things that come clearer to me with every passing year. There is much of the new interpretation that is popular with a number of our modern critics which seems to me just old stuff dressed up in new nomenclature.

I cannot help feeling that styles of theology come and go. As far as belonging to some particular school, I have no ambition at all. Following a rather zigzag trail, theology is nearly always overemphasizing one aspect of the discipline and completely understating other very important things. I have sometimes said, if you take the last word in theology which may not completely please you, just wait a while and theology will come back to your position.

We need a firm theological base for all that we say and preach and believe. Modern preachers who have substituted some kind of psychological folderol for sound doctrine are not very much help to anybody. Worst of all are those who are preaching a psychological salvation with no roots deep into Christian experience. I want no part of that, and, if possible, I will stay away from it completely.

What do I really believe and how will my incomplete theology benefit people who are searching for truth?

One thing has seemed to me to be more important and valid with every passing year. I believe with all my heart that Jesus was right. The truth that was found in Jesus Christ seems to me an eternal truth that I can stand on and bet my life on. I find in the New Testament a foundation of truth that I can believe in with all my being.

This will not place me among the professional theologians —it locates the place where my faith begins, it defines the base on which I can stand. When Henry Ward Beecher, in his first great series of Beecher lectures, talked about "truth through personality," he began with an insight that a man must accept if he is to preach. So when I say Jesus was right, I have the place from which I begin.

Jesus understood life, and when he speaks about it, he speaks with truth. His "hard" sayings are usually insights of the truth that every man has to face soon or late. There is a great word in the Gospel of John, "But Jesus did not trust himself to them, because he knew all men and needed no one to bear witness of man; for he himself knew what was in man." (John 2: 24–25.)

There is not to be found in the Gospels an answer to all the problems a man may face in his life, but I have the unshakable conviction that in Jesus Christ, God has given us the essential clues. Some of the mysteries which I see through a glass darkly will never be made clear to me, and that is where faith comes in. In my faith I find confidence to live victoriously with light enough for the next step. That is all any man could ask.

Some things that used to bother me about the gospel and its nature do not strike me now as very important or in any way as central to the human way of life. What do I think about miracles, for example? That has left me almost completely as one of the essential questions I have to solve. Much about the miracles I do not understand. I cannot tell another person what he ought to think about them and how he ought to react to them. I simply have come to the conclusion about Jesus that his life was full of miracles as, indeed, mine is too. I will understand for certain about some of these things one day, but in the meantime I can trust what I do not see.

I think that one of the greatest miracles I observe in the New Testament has to do with the apostle Paul. The way Paul treated the quarrels and small visions of some of the people of those early churches, how he wrestled with the problems he had to face, seems hardly a place to discuss miracles. Yet through the years the church has thought of those notes he wrote as insights and understandings that could form the basis of Scripture for every man. That seems to me miracle enough, and one that hardly anybody notices.

Jesus is something else altogether. He is so complete in his humanity and so revealing of the mind of God. He speaks the truth in such a way that I can no longer escape it. And what is so amazing, I can know him and have him as my companion and guide. I think he was right and I believe it with all my heart.

It is interesting to note how many things that I thought so important at a certain stage of my life now appear to me to be really a passing phase. To know him and to know Jesus Christ, whom God has sent, now seems to me to be the important thing. This is eternal life and his way of life, and what he tells me about how I ought to live seems to me to have all the authority of God.

With every passing year, the wonder of the incarnation strikes me ever afresh. The Trinity is a hard doctrine to explain, so I do not try at all. It is enough for me to remember what happens to people who deny it. It is a doctrine that I can neither deny nor ignore, because it keeps me close to the mystery of the incarnation. To think that in God's plan there should be a man sent who is more real to me now than he was in the days of his flesh is a wonderful thing indeed. I take great delight in my preaching these days in trying to tell people something of the wonder and the marvel of the incarnation. I do it in terms of bearing witness to what has happened to me and what the incarnation has really come to mean to me because there is no joy like bearing witness to what you believe with all your heart.

I had not been sick at any time in my life until last year. I have now been through a bad time when the Lord has slugged me and made me humble. It has made me understand some things I did not understand before, primarily the reality of the incarnation. I am sick of vague mysticism and tired of trying to make religion a matter of feeling, as some contemporary psychological schools do. I turn to the incarnation as that reality which will save me and keep my mind clear as to the reality of God and of Jesus Christ. I keep free from a vague mysticism and at the same time aware of the hard facts God shares with me about his transcendence. I find the whole business summed up in what the New Testament teaches me about the incarnation. It seems to me that I need this more than anything else.

The Jesus Christ who walked when he was tired, who served men at the same time that he was the Lord of all life, seems to me clear enough evidence about the immanence and the transcendence of God. The clue he gave for understanding his nature is like trying to explain one mystery with another. But we can accept it and believe it. That's the way I feel about it.

I think the highest honor that comes to any man is to preach the gospel. This is where a man works out his theology in the day-by-day, year-in and year-out obligation to stand as a witness to what the gospel means. It is certainly reassuring to know that nothing is going to upset your faith or make you change your mind about what is essential. So I find myself more "sure" about this with every passing day, and it makes me feel sorry for people who are so upset that their religion is always having to be decided now.

I am aware that this point of view may be misunderstood, but I thought I would bear my witness to some of the things that seem to me to be beyond question just now.

I try to keep an open mind toward other religions and I trust that to some extent I succeed. But I am completely committed to being a follower of Christ. I will not argue if you want to be a Buddhist; some of the college students seem to have rediscovered Buddha's way to peace. That will not be my way, because I am a Christian. My belief is that in Jesus Christ God has revealed himself.

So much of this return to religion seems to me to be trying to find something to tickle our fancy. The church is a miracle, and bad as it is at times, it is a place where I work and live. Sometimes I hear a layman criticize the church and I want to say to him, "Move over and give me room." I can usually begin where he stops, for I know more about the church and its weakness than he will ever know.

Still, in all of this I see the "dwelling place of wonder." In the common, ordinary, difficult, and hard things of life I am more convinced than ever that there is a more than human power with whom I can have fellowship and receive my direction.

I am strong for the Bible and read it with increasing appreciation the older I get. The Jewish insight and ideas seem to me to be of lasting significance. I take the prophets' point of view that in working out what justice means for my brethren I am finding Him. I believe that with all my heart.

The way of life presented by the New Testament is utterly realistic. It maintains no sentimental point of view about what man is, nor about the things that last and the things that perish. It always begins with life at its worst, then it comes to the conclusion that there is still an answer and there is still a foundation for faith. I come to this inevitable conclusion that the man who chooses Christ as his guide will not be led on any easy way. With eyes open, we begin with the worst. What a great thing it is to be led by Jesus Christ on the path that always begins by acknowledging evil in all its forms. His way then becomes the way for me, and his way becomes utterly realistic.

A great many of the problems of life seem to spring from failure to take evil seriously. We overlook or we minimize the dangers that might conceivably take place. But the Christian way of life begins by first of all meeting such things head on and assuming that these bad possibilities may be realities we will have to face. It is a great thing to trust our lives to One who first of all begins with the worst.

David H. C. Read

DAVID H. C. READ WAS BORN AT CUPAR, FIFE, SCOT-
land, in 1910. He studied in Montpellier, Strasbourg,
Paris, and Marburg, before receiving his M.A. with
honors from the University of Edinburgh, and his
B.D. from New College.

He was pastor at Coldstream West before becoming a chaplain in the British Army. He was a prisoner
of war from June 1940 until April 1945. He was later
pastor of the Greenback Church of Scotland in Edinburgh, and became the first chaplain of the University
of Edinburgh. From 1952 to 1955, he was Chaplain
to Her Majesty the Queen in Scotland. In 1956 he
became pastor of the Madison Avenue Presbyterian
Church in New York City, where he still serves.

He has served on fact-finding missions to Northern
Ireland and to Moscow, he has been a preacher on
NBC National Radio Pulpit, National Church
Preacher, and a guest speaker for "Jesus Week" at
Columbia University. He has given the Lyman
Beecher Lectures at Yale, the Staley Lectures at Carson-Newman College in Tennessee, the Perkins Lectures at Wichita Falls, Texas, and the Croall Lectures
at Edinburgh. He has published more than twenty
books, the most recent of which are: *Overheard, Curious Christians, An Expanding Faith,* and *A Man Sent
from God.*

God's Grace
Is My Mainspring

DAVID H. C. READ

ONE OF THE OCCUPATIONAL HAZARDS OF THE MINISTRY IS BEING professionally involved with intimate matters of belief. If one is constantly speaking and writing about "holy things," there is a danger of repeating thoughts about God, prayer, faith, and the devotional life which may not always accord with the state of one's own soul. I am not speaking of any conscious hypocrisy but of the inevitable difficulty in sorting out that which passes for belief in the grooves of the mind from that which is real inside. This is what I am now trying to do.

Any search for an expression of my inmost convictions must lead to some autobiography, for it is from formative experiences in the past that present beliefs are distilled. As we get older, certain influences and incidents come into perspective, and we begin to see why we are what we are. Since the substance of this confession will be that the grace of God is the mainspring of my spiritual life, I am really here following Paul —at a respectful distance—saying, "By the grace of God I am what I am" (I Cor. 15:10).

I was raised in what might be called a moderately religious family. My parents were church members but were not "active participators." I never went to Sunday school, but I was introduced to the mysteries of Presbyterian worship at an early age. My chief recollection of this is an objection to being dressed up for the occasion and experiencing considerable boredom during the sermon. I have quite distinct memories of adding to the elementary prayers taught me by my mother some quite specific requests—one of which (for my removal from the class of a teacher I detested) seemed to me to be miraculously granted. This incident impressed me with the possibilities of really talking to God, and I devoured, at an early age, religious books and tracts which a devout Scottish aunt and a grimly pious Irish grandmother put into my hands.

My teen-age years were passed in a state of religious indifference flavored with some active adolescent agnosticism, nourished by writers like Shaw and Wells. My first lively spiritual experience came to me at the age of seventeen in the context of a summer camp for boys. Enticed to this camp by an evangelically-minded friend (whose mind and interests I admired but whose religion I distrusted), I became gripped by the person of Christ. The sense of his reality and nearness as a living force has remained with me in varying degrees of intensity ever since. This was not a "sudden conversion"—it seemed rather the dawning of something I had really known all along —but it was my first experience of what I now call "grace." By it I mean a dependence on God and a trust in Christ which —when I am really on the beam—liberates me from religious anxieties, self-absorption, and worries about the future.

The next enduring mark on my religious life was my call to the ministry. It was, in fact, the only sudden and life-changing experience I have known, and it has undoubtedly determined many of the convictions that I hold today. At the time, I was in the middle of a course in English literature and language at the University of Edinburgh and had no thoughts whatsoever of becoming a minister. One evening I drifted into a church of another denomination. I don't remember who the minister was or anything at all of what he said in the course of his sermon, but I do know that somewhere in the middle of it an overwhelming conviction came to me that I was meant to be a preacher.

Whatever hidden motives may have been operating in me at the time, whatever the temptations to roam in other directions, I have never lost the conviction of this "call." My convictions today about the sovereignty of God and the divine overruling have to do with this experience; I identify easily with the Biblical accounts of the prophet's call where a sense of reluctance and insufficiency combines with an overwhelming and ineluctable divine summons. (Cf. Jer. 1:5–7; 20:7–9.)

The next formative period for my personal faith was during my seminary training when I was adjusting my "evangelical" outlook to my humanistic training, my pietism to my enjoyments, and my belief in the Word of God to Biblical criticism. It began with a year in the Protestant seminaries of France during which a lot of this adjusting took place. What I remember most vividly of that year was a retreat conducted by Pierre Maury. He came to us from Bonn, where he had been absorbing the teachings of Karl Barth. We were intoxicated by the new theology of the Word. Maury's exposition lighted a fire in me that has never gone out, and Barth's theology (however much it was modified by H. R. Mackintosh, John Baillie, and other great teachers at Edinburgh) gave me both a resolution of some agonizing conflicts and a mystical (may Barth forgive me) sense of the glory of God. From then on I have never ceased to be inspired by the mixture of scholarship and passion that animates the greatest theologians and preachers.

All this heady theology had to be brought to earth before I found the working faith about which I am trying to write. This happened, of course, when I found myself in charge of a little country church, but a more drastically winnowing experience awaited me. I became a chaplain in the British Army and served with the Highland Division. Within a few months, during the disastrous campaign in France in 1940, we found ourselves surrounded by Rommel's tanks and guns in the little seaport town of St. Valery in Normandy. At one point I was in a street crammed with troops, fires at each end of the street, awaiting the next salvo from the enemy artillery. That was when the winnowing of beliefs took place, for I was almost certain that I had only a few minutes left to live.

I discovered then what I really believed. It seemed as though all kinds of beliefs that I had previously thought enormously important dropped away and I was left with one central conviction. It came in the form of a text of Paul: "My God shall supply all your need according to his riches in glory by Christ Jesus" (Phil. 4:19). The conviction remained that I was in the hands of God whether I lived or died. It is still my basic working belief to live by and to pass on. That, and the certainty that in Christ God can bring good out of any circumstance at all, and the trust that nothing can separate us from his love.

That experience left me with an enduring sense of God's grace, and also with a certain impatience for all forms of religious fanaticism or excessive scrupulosity. Thus for the ensuing five years, which I spent in prison camps, I was sustained by this grace and realized at the same time the inadequacy of much of our contemporary piety. My sense of an overruling Providence was naturally reinforced when my liberation from a Stalag in the western part of Germany occurred at three o'clock on Good Friday afternoon, 1945.

To disinfect this narrative from any suspicion of what the troops call: "Bother you, Jack, *I*'m all right" (amended), let me add that I accept Peter's word that "God has no favorites." In battle I was never able to use the verse of the psalm that says: "A thousand shall fall at thy side and ten thousand at thy right hand; but it shall not come nigh thee" (Ps. 91:7).

Subsequent experiences of life, personal and public, have reinforced the effects of these formative years. Deeper knowledge of both joy and suffering, wider experience of life in different parts of the world, the demands of an exacting daily schedule, further reading and appreciation of the arts, acceptance of my limitations, unflagging hopes of being a better disciple, dealing with varying moods, new friendships and new discoveries, adjustment to advancing age—all these things are still illuminated for me by the presence of God's grace in Christ. I find myself questioning all kinds of accepted patterns of Christian thoughts and action, but never this inner core. I still am captivated by the combination of the rational and the passionate in the gospel of Christ, and I am stimulated continually by the possibilities of living by grace.

The faith by which I try to live has divinity in it, and I love the catechism definition of the chief end of man. Somewhere for me in the daily round is the vision of glorifying God and enjoying him forever—with a new accent on the "enjoy." But I believe increasingly that this faith has humanity in it too. Love takes on deeper meaning as I realize the humanity of our God. So I want the churches humanized, theology humanized.

I suppose one would have to say that behind all the complications of life, beyond all the sophistications of theology, philosophy, politics, and social contracts, and in spite of frustrations, acedia, and times of spiritual torpor, I have a rather simple trust in a very personal God to whom I speak and from whom I receive both my orders and the reinforcement of his grace.

Erik Routley

ERIK ROUTLEY WAS BORN IN BRIGHTON, ENGLAND, IN
1917. He attended Lancing College in Sussex, and
holds the B.D., M.A., and D.Phil. degrees from Oxford. He is a Fellow of the Royal School of Church
Music and of the Westminster Choir College in the
United States.

He has held pastorates in Dartford, in Edinburgh,
and is currently pastor of St. James United Reformed
Church in Newcastle upon Tyne. From 1948 to 1959
he was a lecturer in church history, director of music,
and chaplain to students at Mansfield College, Oxford. He has been president of the Congregational
Church in England and Wales, and is president of the
Incorporated Association of Organists.

Among his numerous published works are *Creeds
and Confessions, Hymns Today and Tomorrow, Music
Leadership in the Church, Words, Music and the
Church,* and *Exploring the Psalms.* He has also edited
Cantate Domino and since 1948 has been editor of
the *Bulletin of the Hymn Society.*

Something New Every Day

I REMEMBER WELL THAT TRAIN JOURNEY IN 1943. AT THE time, I was still a student in seminary, traveling from London to Manchester to visit the lady who has since become my wife. By some strange providence (it was wartime, of course) I found an empty compartment in the train and I settled down to do some study in preparing a sermon. So it came about that this character with the solemn and zealous face caught me red-handed with a Bible open on the seat as he came in and joined me.

He was one of those persons who tend to ask perfect strangers curious questions. He said abruptly, "Are you a saved man?" I answered, "I believe so." There followed a long and threatening speech from him, because my answer was not what he wanted. I thought the answer not too bad, but with some people you can't win. He said, "You ought to *know.*" Well, after talking back and forth for a time, I think we established some sort of understanding because he said, when we got to Manchester, that we should meet in heaven. I am doing my best to view that prospect with pleasure.

After thirty years, I still claim that my answer was right. Anyhow, I'd give it again if asked the same question. Yes, I do believe. I think that's a much more important statement than saying "I know." Faith is far more interesting than certainty: and Paul didn't say "Certainty, hope, and charity," did he? The way I see it, belief means a contact with something that constantly surprises me, that says something new to me every day. Knowledge is something to be filed away for use when required; faith can't be filed away. It grows and alters and judges and astonishes all the time.

What role has my faith played in my work? How do you expect a minister of the gospel to answer that? You might well say that a minister is paid to have faith, but I don't see it that way. I need personal faith as much in my work as any layman needs it in his. How has faith helped in my day-to-day living? I'd prefer somebody else answered that—my wife, say, or my congregation, or my children. I don't know what sort of job I've made of this; but so far as I can judge, I think I'd have been even more intolerable to live with if I hadn't had this faith.

May I tell you, then, what this faith is—this thing that is always surprising and alerting me? This thing which no doubt I'm constantly resisting and ignoring, but which I'm so glad I've been given?

The story divides into three obvious sections: how I got it, what I got, and what keeps it going.

I'm fortunate—so my story isn't interesting. I had intelligently godly parents, a good home church, and a fascinating religious education. You mustn't congratulate me, but you may envy me if you like. I always hated Sunday school and, even as a child, to some extent enjoyed church. The one part of church I've always resisted is Sunday school. That was my bit of rebellion. I was carried out howling from Sunday school at the age of six. Quite rightly too. I guess they were singing a type of hymn which even then I found revolting. I've been exposed since I was six (wisely, without oppressive talk about duty) to the public worship of the church—which then included forty-minute sermons. That was a tough diet. I consider it fortunate that I was sent away to two Anglican boarding schools, from ages eight to eighteen, where the emphasis wasn't on rousing sermons but on liturgy and the kind of worship in which youngsters could really participate. When I was about fourteen I was spending two thirds of my life observing the delightful routine of Anglican worship and one third being opposed to the stimulating and athletic worship of the Reformed tradition.

My parents were musical and I've always loved the church's music—that's where the Anglicans really got to me. I was at that period when things happen for better or worse in a youngster's life. In the spring of 1934, at the age of sixteen, I was enjoying the aesthetics of the church more than its dogma. The Anglicans were winning. Our church was without a minister, and a visitor came to preach. At last the gospel, as preached, reached me. I remember it like yesterday. I said to my father, "I'm coming again for evening service." It was a fair cop, as we say in England. I was caught. This man—it wasn't only what he said but what he was: the whole person who came rushing at me from the pulpit. I was captivated. Through him I became whatever sort of servant of Christ I am. Because of him I said, "That's a job I'd like to be doing." Because of him I stayed in the Reformed tradition, and I'm there still. I needn't mention his name, because it isn't well known. But he's still alive (eighty-six or so); and he's so modest and good-humored that I doubt if he knows what he did for me, although I've tried to tell him.

So I was launched into a ministry that has given me many surprises and a normal quota of heartaches since I entered it thirty years ago. And the way I came into it, and found Christ, has made it necessary for me always to say that I didn't *do* any of this. Christ did it—heaven knows I grant that—but he used other human beings to do it, and I'm particularly conscious that I've always needed other people. I have always been urged on to the next step of faith by others.

Let me talk now about my favorite subject: what I believe. Broadly speaking, I can say I believe every word, as faithfully as any fundamentalist, of the Nicene Creed. I almost say that that document couldn't have expressed my belief better if I had written it myself. But what I mean by that impudent remark is simply that if I've wanted to objectify my belief, that creed has never let me down. It's far and away better than the so-called Apostles' Creed. A part of my professional life, teaching church history on a campus at Oxford from 1948 to 1959, was devoted to finding out just what the Nicene Creed means. But this statement is to be made in personal terms, so here it is.

First, I love and enjoy the Bible. I revere the scholars who tell me what it's all about. (Actually, I revere some of them, because some don't tell me that at all!) I have a few writers who are my anchors in matters of doctrine, and George Caird is the man I completely trust in Biblical matters. The Bible is a living and exciting book for me. Nathaniel Micklem, my principal in seminary, first taught me how to love it; John Marsh, my teacher and later my colleague, continued the process. I love, and in a sense I believe, every word of it. I don't use it like a telephone directory. I read it as a book about people and about God's ways with them. I'm unspeakably grieved by the ignorance and distrust of the Old Testament that I find so widely in my Britain and in America.

To me, Jesus Christ is what he said he was—God made visible. If I want to know who runs the universe, who is in charge of my life, I can turn to Jesus. Here was the man who said that everything in the Old Testament was the Word of God, but that almost everybody then alive had misinterpreted and perverted it. (Matt. 5:17.) I'm not a fundamentalist, but I love it as much as Billy Graham does, and if I ever meet him (which I'd love to do, though I've disagreed often enough with his conclusions), I believe he'd let me say so. Jesus Christ to me is the person who offers what really does absorb all the energy of my intelligence and devotion. He's the living authentication of joy and victory.

But next, I find myself saying something with which some people don't seem to agree. I believe that Jesus Christ wants me not only to believe in him but also to believe in his Father. I can't get anything else out of the Gospels. He wants me to believe that what he did (in miracles, teachings, sacrifice, resurrection) is a picture of what God is constantly doing, timelessly doing, in the world.

This is terribly important to me. If I just believed in Jesus, I could be believing in a marvelous man who did things and then went away. But I'm required, and I rejoice, to believe in a God—an author and finisher of everything visible and invisible—who has all the passion and joy and courage and glory that we saw in Jesus. I do really believe that Jesus wanted us not to spend all our time praising him, but to come to a total view of life that springs from a new belief about God, the Father, Son, and Holy Spirit. I believe that not doing this, but believing that God doesn't love the world, is sin. It is possible to believe that Jesus came to set right a world which God had allowed to get into a mess; that Jesus loves people but God doesn't. To me that is blasphemy. Just think of that cripple in John 5:5–14, how easily he could have said, "God made me a cripple; Jesus made me whole." But Jesus said, "Sin no more, don't go on saying I'm marvelous; get right with God."

Going on from there, I believe that after the crucifixion and resurrection of Jesus (I'm a Reformed Christian: I can't separate those two!) the Holy Spirit came. What happened when he came was that ordinary men found they could do Christ's work without having Jesus physically by their side directing them (John 14:12; 16:7). In the church we've been doing that ever since: forgiving sin (which is the same as reconciling men to the Father), proclaiming eternal life here and now, generating friendship.

I must press on. What I've been saying is personal rather than general. It is what I try to preach: God loves the world and always did. Change your attitude toward God as Jesus has taught you and you'll get the message. I know there are some consequences that are mine and need not be yours.

What I can never forget is the debt I owe to other people. I have written a number of books and preached a lot of sermons and yet I have never had an idea that I didn't owe to somebody else. When a man says to me that he's self-taught, I either disbelieve him or have to say, It can't happen to me. I've been receiving new confirmations of the gospel, new corrections of my own attempts at belief, every day of my life, and I'm now pushing fifty-six. Wise and simple people in my congregation, writers and artists, friends at college, teachers and pastors, every one of them leaves me different from the way he found me. Some of them work changes that are painful but for which I'm now grateful—like surgery or diet. One of my favorite stories in the Bible is in Acts where that famous preacher Apollos fired off a thundering sermon. He was told over lunch by those good lay people Aquila and Priscilla that it was all very impressive but it wasn't the gospel (Acts, chs. 18; 19). How I've needed my Aquilas and Priscillas!

It comes to this. I have thirty years of ministry to look back on, and humanly speaking it has all been energized and made fruitful, not by me but by the Lord speaking through my friends, many of whom live in the United States. I've never had reason to go back on my faith; they've just confirmed the faith when they corrected and rebuked me.

My brief for this article includes some account of my doubts. You'll have to believe me when I say that most of what I read and hear about doubts seems quite foreign to my own experience. I respect Thomas (John, ch. 20): I respect the man who won't be fooled, who won't switch off his intellect. I fear and resist the anti-intellectualism of so many in the contemporary church. I look with alarm and sometimes grief at the antics of people who place such a great reliance on doubt. I remember that preposterous "death of God" controversy of 1966 which broke while I was in the United States. My view is that Christ isn't mocked by any of this, but that it's time people grew up. You grow up to faith, not to doubt.

What should I say about doubt? That I doubt the resurrection of the body or something? Good heavens! All I need is there in I Cor. ch. 15, which gives no ground for a naïve or self-deluding belief in resurrection. On the contrary, it spells out quite exactly what resurrection is. Should I say I doubt the existence of an afterlife? I'll say I know nothing about it, and I believe we aren't supposed to know anything about it, God reserves some surprises for us even after death. Heaven and hell? I know enough about those to go along. Heaven is the presence of Christ and hell is his absence. Hell is self-chosen loneliness: it's what you get, because you asked for it, when you say to God, "I don't want your charity." I'd give all I have to deliver my friends from that. It's like suddenly being separated from the person you most love, and knowing that you positively and directly asked to be so separated. That's hideous enough for me.

No. I don't happen to think it's clever to analyze the Christian faith, to find out how much one personally disagrees with. Our Lord's moral system (Matt., chs. 5 to 7) was a celebration of the beauty of goodness, not of the horror of badness. Don't do good to escape hell: do good because those who do it are happy—that's exactly what he said. Intellectually it's the same for me. If I owe more to one writer than to another, it's to C. S. Lewis that I most often turn. He said somewhere, "If there's a part of the faith you find it difficult to believe, work on it: that's the part you most need to believe." That's the line I try to take.

So you see, this article may be the most useless one in this book, because I'm a receiver, not a giver. In passing on what Christ has given me, I'm five percent efficient at best. But at least I do know what I've received. And I've received it—how else can it come?—through Christ's church, through my friends and teachers and preceptors that the church has provided. I'll receive more from the new friend I meet tomorrow.

One final statement will disqualify me for good from being a fashionable theologian. I find it absolutely impossible to be a Christian without the church, and I mean the visible, institutional church. I mean the church *I didn't choose.* I mean the church that God gave me for my home. If I had to choose my teachers, my friends, my authorities, what a jejune and barren life I should lead! But here's the church, with all these people I didn't choose, and all these doctrines I didn't think up, and all this discipline I didn't invent. It's always the things and people I didn't choose that did me most good. "You have not chosen me, but I have chosen you." (John 15:16.) I don't plan too much; there are all these people, and above them all there is Christ, to do that for me. So I don't have to take myself too seriously, or to be too anxious. Left to myself I think I can see how impossible I would have been. If I'm tolerable as a minister or a person, it's because of all this that was given to me.

Frederick Sontag

FREDERICK SONTAG WAS BORN IN LONG BEACH, CALI-
fornia, in 1924. He was graduated from Stanford University with majors in psychology and philosophy, and
received his M.A. and Ph.D. degrees from Yale in the
field of philosophy.

His first teaching experience was as an instructor at
Yale. Since 1952 he has been professor of philosophy
at Pomona College. He has served as visiting lecturer
at Union Theological Seminary in New York, at the
Pontifical College of San Anselmo in Rome, and at
the University of Copenhagen.

Among other memberships and activities, he be-
longs to Phi Beta Kappa, the American Philosophical
Association, the Metaphysical Society of America, the
Society for Religion in Higher Education, and the
Kent Fellowship Program of the Danforth Founda-
tion. His many books include *The Crisis of Faith, The
God of Evil, God, Why Did You Do That?, How
Philosophy Shapes Theology,* and *The American Reli-
gious Experience.*

Finding God with Us

To render an account of faith should always require us to give a personal history, since faith never springs full blown. It is always acquired over a period of time and by a series of changes. Furthermore, faith is never one thing for all, the same in every time and place. It is true that men have long been trying to make faith uniform, to force it to be one and the same for all. The history of religious persecution indicates that faith, as it springs up naturally, is far from uniform. There is no reason to think that God cannot deal with such individuality and heterodoxy, but this natural confusion has upset men for centuries.

Thus, if we want to understand what faith is, rather than what men wish it were for their own convenience, we must listen afresh to the testimony of each individual and expect a new account in each future case. This is not to say that we do not have classic examples of faith (e.g., Paul or Augustine), or that there is not much that is similar and shared by all believers. However, if we are to understand faith, we must always be prepared to hear a new story, particularly if we want to find faith in our own time and not just know what it has been like before. If we accept the amazing diversity of faith, we realize that God has not worked for our convenience or cared about our desire to control. Rather, he has preferred to express the variety and depth of his own nature by affecting men in ever new ways.

Furthermore, faith must involve an account of how it arrived in any given situation, because it always has the aspect of a gift. No matter how hard we work for it, if faith arrives, it is simply one day discovered to have come to us on its own terms, not on ours. This does not necessarily mean that the ability to believe is given to those who do not seek it or to those who do nothing to uncover it. Developing faith may require a great deal on our part, perhaps even a long pilgrimage, but it is never coerced or forced to appear by our action. Often it arrives in unexpected ways and times. Thus, there is a mystery story aspect in every account of faith. We cannot guess who is the hero and who is the villain until the story reaches its climax. We appreciate what is given to us more than what we control, although we feel safer with the latter and freer with the former.

Faith may settle down on a grown man who is secular to his core with no previous experience in religion. God may act as he chooses, yet by all accounts such unexpected conversions are rare. Thus, we often must go back to our childhood to account for faith, and those years were not governed by our own choosing. We had to receive what we were given before we could become able to judge it. So much of the struggle of faith in later years concerns either appropriating or rejecting what we had been given in those years before we were responsible. Many times we consider childhood religion as representing that against which we must rebel. Actually it is the very model of what faith is (if only we could accept it as such) just because it was given to us rather than selected. That is why faith requires a constant return to the ways of childhood.

In one sense the coming of faith always gives new life; that is, it cannot infuse those who are old in spirit but only those who can constantly reappropriate their youth. It is hard to say whether faith comes because we can turn young again, or whether we are released from time because faith arrived and enabled us to become young in spirit. Thus we see the irony of those who reject their childhood religious faith. They push away just the situation that must be recovered. This is not to say that we must all once again believe just what we once did at an earlier age without further reflection or choice. It is just that the situation of youth is the condition for the return of faith, no matter how much more mature or experienced the intervening years have made us.

In an unknowing sense, God may be with little children. Thus when faith arrives later, we may in a real sense become as children once again, although perhaps in a more conscious way this time. I am not suggesting that every child experiences God or that all childhood is so delightful that we should want to return to it. Some children feel so lonely and miserable that they never wish to experience childhood again if they can prevent it. Still, childhood at its best is an attitude that both receives without resistance and accepts care openly and gratefully. Both are prime requisites of faith. As with all experience, our task may be to retain and to revive the best aspects of our childish years without letting the negative factors blind us as to what we should still select and preserve.

If faith, then, is to *discover that God is with us,* the question arises as to how this happens to us and what it means when it does. Is God literally and visibly with us? That cannot be, and his natural inability to appear as a discernible object has led many to disbelieve in his power to appear at all. It is this restriction on divinity which leads to the very necessity for faith itself. One can only "believe" what one cannot see directly. If this is true, can God come to us? If so, what is such an appearance like? He may be present in things seen: he himself is just not seen there, although his actions may be. It is only as a result of something we do or see or feel that we are ever moved to declare God's presence. This usually happens as the result of a sudden change, an alteration otherwise unexpected, whose felt force seems to require a nonnatural power or cause.

Such realization need not come all at once or only from a suddenly changed condition. Quite often the realization is grasped in retrospect because God remains unseen, but in looking back we become aware of a presence moving with us. His disciples, for instance, seldom recognized Jesus for what he was and his actions for what they were. Later, in realizing what had happened to their lives, they came to assert God's powerful presence working among them. We have similar experiences particularly in situations in which our life is renewed outside nature's normal ways. Where God appears, life overflows, although this may require both confrontation and destruction as a prelude and often the process remains incomprehensible at the time.

My father was a Jew, the son of a rabbi, one who came to America from Russia to escape the persecution that destroyed his family. With no Jewish community in the little California town in which he settled, he attended church with the Baptist family who befriended him. Finally when he could understand the message preached to him, he received the Word and was baptized. He was, then, "an original Christian," i.e., a trained and orthodox Jew who heard the proclamation of the gospel and accepted Jesus as the Christ, the Savior, long promised to the Jews. He was changed in this experience and he could never forget it. It became his faith and the foundation of his future. His sins were forgiven and his life was placed on a new basis. God had again made himself available to man.

My mother was a Methodist who grew up in an Iowa country town, of German immigrant parents. She accepted her Protestantism as she did her own American heritage. My father always refused to discuss the Old World and his old religion, in whose eyes he was now dead. So it is not by much discussion that this background became known but only by reflective inference. His life was new, but in his later years his Jewish heritage returned to him more and more as illness and the troubles of the economic depression set in. The origins of his faith returned to him more strongly with age and difficulty, as they will to us all, but he never rejected the new life he had found.

If I was not born in the Baptist church, at least I made my first public appearance there, and its life structured the pattern of much of my early years. I do not now believe exactly what I believed then. Yet I was not warped by those early years but rather was given a base from which to work out the future. To give an account of one's growth to date is never to define faith fully, for the story of faith is not over until life is over. To live in faith means to be prepared for change, even when the time for change seems long past, as it did for Abraham. Thus, a definition of faith must be a posthumous work, and in that sense it is impossible for a man to write it while he lives. Yet he can see where it came from, what it has come to mean, how he sees God in the light of the changes in his life, and then declare how he stands ready to receive the future. Since faith happens to us, it is never contained by us. Yet it is possible to determine its base and to declare its presence.

Those who reject their parents and their ways have a harder time in the life of religion. This is not because we need to believe or act as our family did, but because by rejection we divorce ourselves from what should form the basis for later reflection. In that sense, the search for faith is always in part the search for a lost childhood, for faith involves accounting for how it began. We turn back to find a new way forward. Faith is never needed unless one is blocked in growth in his present life. In that case, the only way to find a new direction is to examine our origins once again.

While I was in my teens it was taken for granted that I would become a Baptist minister. My father hoped for that, since he had not been able to continue the family rabbinical traditions, and I accepted a ministerial goal as natural. I learned the books of the Bible by heart, as well as many of the more famous New Testament verses. I went to church camps, revivals, prayer meetings, and two Sunday services as well as Sunday school. We said grace at meals, to be sure, and our family attended religious services regularly, but little was spoken of religion in the house, although much was assumed.

My father, for instance, never discussed his Jewish background or took us to a synagogue, although on occasion he went at holiday season himself, drawn irresistibly by a lost past. Still, he was essentially of the New World and of a new religion and he said the past belonged to an Old World. My father was a quiet but prominent figure in our First Baptist Church. I knew of his religious attachment more by the way he sang hymns and the emotion I could feel while I was sitting next to him than by anything he ever said. In the manner in which some families use religion as a topic for household debate, I never knew it in my home. Religion was something to be felt, to act upon and respond to, more than to discuss. To argue my way either into or out of religion never occurred to me. I had been born to it, and it was mine.

My Baptist minister warned me that if I persisted in my wish to go to Stanford instead of to the University of Redlands, which was Baptist sponsored, I would not become a minister. Indeed, his prediction was correct, although I do not think the reason I was never ordained is to be found in Stanford. It was inevitable that, as I left the small coastal town in California, all sorts of new influences would be brought to bear upon my life and ways. My gradual but increasing involvement in the pursuit of philosophy was all but inevitable. In its approach I found the kind of attack on problems with which I had always been sympathetic but had never known. Thus began a long tension between the roles of philosophy and religion in my life. Yet this tension never became destructive but rather the source of what fruitfulness I have professionally.

At the same time, an inevitable companion tension arose over what professional calling I would follow. My minister was right that seminary would not remain an assumed goal, but again not because of new secular pressures but because I came to be aware of a much wider avenue of service. I had never considered teaching, yet now it appeared as a natural avenue. So it has been, and I think it has been a form of ministry too. Yet the possibility of ordination has never disappeared but keeps suggesting itself from time to time. I enjoy an opportunity to preach, and it is true that there is little great preaching today. Yet the barriers to faith lie more on intellectual frontiers today, and it is there that the call still seems to me to be most urgent.

I cannot say that I ever went through the dramatic doubts of atheism, as advertised by so many, nor did I ever grow hostile about the church's institutional shortcomings. Since I was

never terribly cynical nor overly optimistic about what to expect from either institutions or professionals in religion, I never
expected too much and thus was not subject to wide cycles of
disappointment. A time came when my life was caught up in
a whirl of secular and intellectual concerns. They were sufficient to keep me both busy and content, and this new life left
me little time to reflect on an earlier simple life. A former faith
was not really lost or ostentatiously rejected; it merely receded
into the background for a time.

Then, one day it reappeared slowly and quietly. As I followed
the struggles of others, often my students, I rhetorically asked
myself whether I should continue to be religiously interested.
I discovered—with a humorous touch in the realization—that
I really did not have a choice in the matter. I was religious both
by nature and by inheritance, and there was not much I could
do about it except to avoid the obvious by hiding it. I am now
convinced that most of us find "God with us" in just this sort
of way if we ever do. Christianity is, or should be, used to the
idea of God's unexpected appearance. We struggle, we reject,
we avoid by preoccupation, but God's appearance to us is never
in the way of our choice or under our control. If we are to be
graced by God's presence, it is likely to be in a manner and a
time not of our own choosing.

It takes only half a lifetime to realize that faith never comes,
and is never given, all at once. Paul might have thought so,
because of the Damascus road conversion. But his further
experience after that dramatic event proved to him that God's
appearance was only the beginning of a divine learning process
and not the end. So it seems to me. Faith now means a
willingness to wait for life's unfolding and to see what lies in
store. Faith means a relaxation of control and the forfeiture of
any demand for assurance now. When faith is accepted this
way, then all that one does not know is no longer such a bother.
Then one becomes willing to wait in obedience to see what link
between God and man will unfold. Such a mood offers no
guarantee of completeness in any lifetime, but it is an enormous relief in contrast to the immense burden of constantly

trying to see if now one can at last be certain and be done with it.

Such a life of faith is a willingness to trust God to the end, "though he slay me." It does not mean that one's immediate wishes are fulfilled or that all accumulated intellectual puzzles are suddenly solved against their reappearance. Faith is an acceptance of change or a promise of more than a present fulfillment. Yet one becomes young in such a process just because he is constantly oriented toward a future that is not here, rather than always demanding satisfaction in the present or moaning over a past. Faith of this kind is not one's own to control in its coming and going. To cease to try to regulate it may be the best demonstration of faith's presence.

Frank Stagg

FRANK STAGG WAS BORN IN EUNICE, LOUISIANA, IN 1911. He attended Louisiana College, and received his Th.M. and Ph.D. degrees from Southern Baptist Theological Seminary in Louisville, Kentucky. He has pursued advanced study at Union Theological Seminary in New York, the University of Edinburgh, the University of Basel, and the University of Tübingen.

He was pastor of the First Baptist Church in De-Ridder, Louisiana, before joining the faculty of Southern Baptist Theological Seminary in Louisville, where he is currently James Buchanan Harrison Professor of New Testament Interpretation.

His scholarly endeavors include the collating of thirteenth-century Greek manuscripts of Luke for the Textual Criticism project as well as a number of books that have been translated into other languages. His recent books include *Studies in Luke's Gospel* and *Polarities of Man's Existence in Biblical Perspective.* He is consulting editor to The Broadman Bible Commentary, to which he has contributed volumes on Matthew and Philippians.

145

A Continuing Pilgrimage

FRANK STAGG

CHOOSING ONE'S PARENTAGE IS NOT AN OPTION GIVEN TO US, but I have no regrets about mine. Surely there were minuses along with the pluses in the home into which I was born and which had so much to do with my formative years, but the pluses were far more significant for me than the minuses. To this day, the foundations for my faith and my values are to be found in that home, housed on a rice farm in Acadia Parish in Louisiana.

My parents, now deceased, could hardly have anticipated some of the positions with respect to theology and positions with respect to social issues to which I gradually came, through much anguish. Yet there is a strong continuity between what they taught me by word, example, and conclusions that I eventually reached, even though these conclusions were not anticipated by them nor by me in earlier days. It was the logic of much they taught me that drove me to reassess my world of thought, theology, and practice. Had they lived on to know some of the advantages that came to me in the changing and larger world than they had opportunity to know—their travels were but a few hundred miles in length—they too may have been driven to some of the reassessments and readjustments experienced by their sons and daughter. I will not fault them for what they did in and with their circumstances; I do thank them for what they gave me: a basic orientation and a faith that required somewhat painful correcting and redirecting, but that has not required abandonment. The road they started me on in theological faith and in ethical value was not a dead-end street. It has lead to unanticipated openings and journeys.

Our farm home was not a home of many books, and there was no accessible library. The few books that we had, however, were significant. Beyond the shadow of a doubt, the Bible was for us *the Book*. I never heard terms such as "infallible," "inerrant," or "verbal inspiration," in my home. The Bible was never defended, for it was not on trial. The atmosphere of the home was such that one under its influence simply assumed the basic nature and trustworthiness of the Bible. There were no fixed times for reading or discussing it, and there was no aware-ness of such a need. The Bible was read normally and regularly, not as a chore to perform but as a source of guidance and strength to which we turned. It was the church, not the home, that taught us that it was a *duty* to read the Bible, and this probably did more harm than good, making the Bible an object of worship, or the focus of a painful task rather than a spring from which to drink. My home did more than my church in conditioning me for a life of both devotional and critical Bible study.

My mother and father were sufficiently different to make distinct contributions to their children. My mother read the Bible devotedly, but hers was not a scholarly turn, even though her father held a Bachelor of Arts degree from the old Chicago University, with special attention to classical Greek. I still have his 1860 edition of the Liddel and Scott Greek lexicon. Her strength was in her quiet piety, impeccable character, and simple devotion. Among the memories of her that linger was her disposition to believe in people. She could turn off a bad report by saying, "Maybe it isn't so." Her children were at least exposed to this gentle spirit.

My father was a displaced teacher. He grew up on a rice farm and died a rice farmer, but he belonged in the classroom. He could spend hours with a book, but his patience was soon exhausted by a balky mule and he never learned how to cope with a burned-out bearing. He did teach in a one-room school for a few years, but the responsibilities of a growing family

compelled him to turn from the meager opportunities of the
school system to farming, which though not lucrative at least
offered a living. With a strong foundation in mathematics and
Latin, he continued to study within the limits of his situation.
With absolutely no guidance toward critical study of the Bible,
he stumbled upon the beginnings of it through his own initiative and by instinctively applying to Biblical study some of the
principles he had acquired in the disciplines of mathematics
and Latin which he loved so well.

By modern standards my father did not become a critical
scholar. He was a stranger to textual criticism, and anything
like source, form, or redaction criticism was completely outside his world. But his approach to Biblical study was instinctively critical as well as devotional. He did challenge
interpretations and positions that were taken for granted in
the pulpits. He would never sacrifice evidence or reason to
"faith." He did not see faith as something that required
one to stop thinking or asking questions.

I doubt that my father had ever heard about *fides quaerens
intellectum* (faith seeking intelligence), even though he could
read Latin. Incidentally, it is ironic that he was offered a classical education in Latin, but was not introduced to Christian
literature in Latin. The schools had introduced him to Caesar,
Vergil, and Seneca, but the church had not guided him to
Cyprian or Augustine. Nevertheless, he did expose me to some
attitudes which more than any other prepared me to study the
Bible critically as well as devotionally, not as two things but as
one thing. As a young professor, my first major struggle was for
academic freedom, a struggle first with my own fears and then
with obscurantists who, like dogs in the manger, could not eat
the hay and were determined that no one else would. In this
struggle I did not have to abort my father's approach to the
Bible, only enlighten and correct it.

This is not to overlook negative factors in my boyhood
home. We accepted uncritically much that belonged to the
culture of the day, including cultural religion within the
church. For example, we did not question racial segregation.

My father left no doubt about keeping intact the social barriers between the races. He was fluent in French, and so was fully sensitive to the derivation of the nickname borne by the son of a Negro tenant, called "Fra." He knew that *frère* was French for "brother," just as he knew *frater* was Latin for the same. We boys were calling this black boy "Fra," until our father overheard us. We forthwith got a lesson not only in linguistics but also in social relationships. We simply were to call no black person "brother," any more than we were to address any black person as "Mr.," "Mrs.," or "Miss." The blacks were to be kept "in their place," as dictated by culture and as accepted without question or examination by the church. To that extent my parents were culturally and culture-religion determined.

But there was an ambiguity in the racial prejudice and the patterns that my parents inherited and passed on to us. There were some discordant notes within that pattern. There were some unresolved tensions—tensions with which we children were compelled to struggle far more than was ever apparent to us in our parents. Yet the foundations were there, in our home and in our parents. For example, although we were not to call Thales "Fra," neither were we allowed to lay a hand on him or any other black person, however angered by him we might be. It was simply a law, not negotiable. No white person was to strike a Negro under any circumstances. Of course, there were all kinds of motives and complications behind this position, but in it all was the trace of some uneasiness of conscience. These were persons with feelings and value, and they were to be respected—even if only in a patronizing way. My parents did not live to get it straightened out, and possibly they could not have made the adjustment. But they left their children not only a pattern of racial prejudice but also some attitudes, principles, and values that could not escape eventual reassessment and redirection.

The Call to Preach

When I reflect upon my life and try to make some sense of the turns it has taken, I am compelled to see my "call to preach" as foundational and decisive. This experience was far more traumatic and its memory is more vivid than my "conversion" to Christ. Of course, I can recall my commitment to Christ as a boy of eleven years, but this decision was predictable and involved little struggle. The call to preach was neither smooth nor easy. It was an unrelenting trauma that continued for a full year, a private agony shared with no one until suddenly declared openly before my home church.

I say no one, but I should say with no human being. I did pray daily and almost incessantly for a solid year, trying to come to the right decision. It was not a matter of unwillingness to preach; it was that I could not see how I possibly could meet the demands of a preaching ministry. I was timid. I had no experience in public speaking and thought that I had no gifts for it. I had such a high regard for "the ministry," an unwitting compliment to the pastors I had known, that the thought of it frightened me. It just seemed incongruous that I should offer myself for the ministry.

But there was one overriding factor. There was a sense of direction that had come unanticipated by me and that just would not go away. I could not ignore it. I could not put it out of mind. It remained and grew ever more dominating, alongside the bewilderment and fears that haunted me. I had just graduated from high school, and I stayed out of school for a full year. This was the year of trauma. All one fall and winter I worked day after day driving four mules on a "gang plow," plowing the fields for next spring's rice planting. It doesn't take much thinking to keep four mules circling a field, pulling a plow. That left long hours of solitude, day after day, week after week. Seemingly endless hours were concentrated upon one thing—What am I to do with my life? I was not running from anything, at least not consciously. Farming was hard work, but all in all I liked the farm. There was just this strange thought that kept coming back—"Preach."

In addition to the field work were the "chores," at daybreak and again at night. I was milking the cows, for my father was trying on the side to bring in a little cash for the family. While waiting for the cows and calves to finish eating, I had many minutes for meditation. I can yet see the feed sack that served as the "altar" in a feed room that became a prayer room. There through many months my decision was fought through. The public decision must have surprised nearly everyone, including me. At the close of a Sunday morning service I offered myself to the church for ministry. I don't remember really making the decision. It was more like something made for me than made by me. Such experience lends itself to various psychological and sociological interpretations, but for me there has subsequently never been but one explanation. For some strange reason, this is what God wanted me to do. God can speak; he does call; and he can get through to a lad on a farm. This conviction has been the strongest single supportive factor to me in a pilgrimage of faith and in a ministry that at times has been stormy.

I shall always be grateful to my pastor, M. E. Williamson, who gave me understanding and encouragement when I most needed it. He shared his pulpit with me, and the congregation of friends and kinsmen patiently listened to my first preaching efforts. G. Earl Guinn (now president of Louisiana College), my brother Paul, and others also first preached to this congregation.

Shaping a Theology

My formal study of the Bible and theology began in college, but actually it never got beyond the devotional stage there. The time was not lost, however, for there were some values and attitudes of lasting significance for me. Seminary opened new doors and windows. A solid foundation was laid in Hebrew and Greek, and there was something about the faculty and class-

room that made me want to achieve scholarly excellence. The
impact of seminary was solidly on the side of study, not its
neglect. In some areas this was guided very effectively, in others
there was much to be desired.

It was in seminary that I was offered some of the basic tools
for Biblical study, as well as some basic attitudes and principles
for it. What was offered was open-ended. It could be built
upon, corrected, refined. It did not have to be aborted, abandoned, or repudiated.

My seminary days fell in the era when the thinking of its
president, E. Y. Mullins, was so entrenched at the seminary
that there was little opportunity for an optional approach. This
theology was a dead-end street. It was not modified so much
as dropped. Probably its great achievement was in freeing
Southern Baptists from the blight of Calvinism. Without that
liberation Southern Baptists would have been thwarted from
any real evangelism or missions. For that we doubtless owe
Mullins a great debt. But in overcoming the *rigor mortis* of
Calvinism, Mullins developed a theology so tied to a dated
psychology, philosophy, and rationalism that it too died of
suffocation.

Although I never studied with W. T. Conner and saw him
only once, I owe much to him through his writings. Comparison of my *New Testament Theology* with his writings would
reflect considerable independence if not difference, but this is
not to discount my debt to him, especially with respect to the
meaning of the cross.

Probably my pastoral experience provided the greatest impact upon the direction of my theological inquiry. Until 1945
it had never occurred to me that I would serve other than in
the pastorate. Graduate study in the Greek New Testament
was with a pastoral-preaching ministry in mind. I wanted to
bring together the message of the New Testament and the
needs of the people. I found that simply to repeat old lines,
however venerated, had little if any effect upon the people.
Resounding amens to theological propositions did not neces-

sarily imply any significant change in the way people lived. Closer study of Scripture showed that neither Old Testament nor New Testament was primarily concerned with theology as such. The interest there was with the personal: God and man. It was concerned with the relationship people have with one another under God.

In my pastoral ministry I saw that what people required and what Scripture proclaimed was more than theological descriptions of divine transactions. People need the presence of God in their lives, not just theological propositions to which they give assent. No one is saved by theological propositions any more than one is fed by a recipe or a menu. Only the food that is eaten and assimilated nourishes the body. Salvation calls for nothing short of Jesus Christ as a living and transforming presence in the depth of one's existence.

My attention focused in particular on the cross. The fact that Jesus died on a cross two thousand years ago has made little or no difference in the character and life of much of the world. It had no apparent effect upon the life-style of Hitler, Stalin, or countless others who have given themselves to murder, theft, rape, oppression, and the like. It did not keep churchmen from persecuting one another, sometimes even to the point of death. As an event in history it did not hold homes together, or give meaning to individuals. How then does the cross become redemptive? How does what Jesus was and did have saving effect upon any person? That is the question I asked, and the New Testament is clear and compelling in its answer—if we will just let it speak, even if it crushes some of our venerated ideas and theological idols.

I came to see that one is not saved by theology, either good or bad. He is saved by the Savior. He is saved only as the Savior is admitted into his own existence through the openness of faith that is trust. Christ died *for* us, on our account; but more is required of us. We must enter into his dying with him, if he is to save us. We must trust him enough to let him come in and begin to put to death the old egocentric who destroys life in the very act of trying to save it. The paradox is that one lives only by dying. He must be crucified with Christ if he is to live with him.

With this beginning, other doctrines were reexamined, and Scripture was studied afresh. Everywhere new meaning began to appear as the person-centered, the life-centered, the existence-centered nature of Scripture was felt. Movement in this direction got a strong new impetus from John Baillie by virtue of a sabbatical and a cold winter in Edinburgh, Scotland. This pilgrimage is reflected in my writings, should one want to pursue it farther.

Ethical Concern

Theological perspective and ethical concern go together. My awakening to various social and moral issues came slowly and not without considerable anguish, apprehension, pain, and fear. Many contributed to that awakening. My younger brother in the ministry played a significant part in it. Paul went through the same struggles as I, but with less resistance and quicker decision. He was decades ahead of most of his elders and peers on various fronts where Christian conscience should impinge upon social concerns: race relations, open housing, war and peace, poverty and wealth, freedom and dignity for all people. Paul L. Stagg is now secretary for the New Jersey Council of Churches, Newark, New Jersey.

Others helped me awaken to New Testament intention and its implications and applications to social as well as individual change. I first met Clarence Jordan when we were college students, he from Georgia and I from Louisiana, presidents of our state Baptist Student Union conventions. It was then that I heard him tell about his military training and the awakening of his conscience against war. I had never before heard anyone question the rightness of war. He also rejected racial discrimination, something that I had until then not heard challenged in any religious gathering. There was Edward A. McDowell, whom I served as Fellow in Greek in graduate study. He began to relate the New Testament to life situations as I had never heard done before. There were others, also, some of them undergoing struggles paralleling mine, but the persons mentioned are among those who helped me most.

My earliest attempt to do anything serious about race relations was in the pastorate to which I went upon seminary graduation. Barely had I arrived when we were as a nation drawn into World War II. The military was then strictly segregated. Our town was soon flanked by a major army base and an air base, and the whole area was covered by multiplied thousands on maneuvers. At one time a black division was bivouacked just outside our town. Twenty miles away there had been serious interracial incidents. Some of us tried to give our situation a different turn. One result was a service in our church in which a black chaplain and I shared the pulpit and a choral group of black soldiers sang. It was an integrated service—partially integrated, at least, and just one, only one. It was a short step, but it was a step. Months later the record showed that there had not been one incident of racial conflict for that period in the town. But the harder steps—in conversations, in preaching, and in writing—were yet to come. The '40s and '50s were the hard years in the concern for racial justice. There were difficult steps to take, but they had to be taken, and they were taken.

I supported the nation's participation in World War II, but with anguish. It seemed to be the lesser of two evils. Before civilians and the military I pleaded that we not make it a "holy war," even as we did what we thought we must do. Preaching to congregations with as many in uniform as in civilian dress, I warned against letting our "enemy" make us over into his image. Increasingly it has become difficult to justify any war. Somehow, "just wars" turn out to be *just* wars. The best defense we make for participating in war is the judgment that it is the lesser of two evils. On that basis, war is one thing. It is an entirely different thing, however, to kill in the name of Jesus. If we are going to resort to brute force, let's do it in our names, not in his.

Increasingly, in studying the New Testament and especially the Gospels, I have been convinced that salvation is God's work of making us truly human, nothing more and nothing less. To be saved is not to become God, not to become an angel, and not to have life reduced to a fraction or a fragment. It is Christ's work to make the total man well (John 7:23). He laid great emphasis upon sight for the blind, hearing for the deaf, cleansing for the leper, strength for the lame, life for the dead, and the gospel for the poor (Luke 4:16–30; 7:18–23). This means that he was on the side of life, not death; health, not sickness; food for the hungry, not hoarding it all for the favored few. He was on the side of peace, not war. He was on the side of purity, integrity, and humble trust in God, not on the side of arrogance, pride, and self-worship or self-service.

I have also been driven by New Testament study and by increasing awareness of the world's needs to focus my ministry more on the care of God's good earth instead of on pollution and depletion.

To sum it up: the '30s was the decade of finding a basic sense of direction and laying foundations in study and ministry. The '40s brought home to me the trauma of race relations and war. The late '40s and early '50s were the years of struggle with my own mind and conscience for academic integrity and with obscurants for freedom to read, to write, and to speak. The middle '60s brought to crushing force the issues of war and peace which had been only partially awake since the early '40s. The late '60s brought the "moment of truth" about ecology, with our gross guilt of sin against nature and the absolute demand that our course be reversed. All along the way was concern for the poor, in part because I lived through the Depression in the '30s and in part because one can hardly wear the covers off many Greek New Testaments without finally becoming sensitized to its great concern for the material as well as the higher needs of mankind.

Helmut Thielicke

HELMUT THIELICKE WAS BORN IN BARMEN IN 1908. His early studies at Greifswald, Marburg, Erlangen, and Bonn were frequently interrupted by long stays in clinical hospitals. He was awarded the Ph.D. degree by the University of Erlangen in 1931, and became professor of theology at the University of Heidelberg in 1936. Because of his outspoken views concerning the relationship of church and state he was expelled from that position in 1940.

He became pastor of the Lutheran church in Ravensburg with restriction on travel and writing. He then became head of the Theological Office of the Württemberg Church, and in 1945 was professor of systematic theology at the University of Tübingen. In 1954 he moved to the same chair at the University of Hamburg, where he still serves. He has honorary degrees from the Universities of Heidelberg and Glasgow, and was awarded the Great Cross for services to the Republic of Germany.

His writing has been prolific, totaling over seventy titles. His works have been translated into twelve languages. Among those available in English are his two-volume work entitled *Theological Ethics, Nihilism: Its Origin and Nature with a Christian Answer, The Trouble with the Church, I Believe: The Christian's Creed,* and *Death and Life.*

God Reached
Into My Life

HELMUT THIELICKE
Translated by Dr. James L. Blevins

As a small boy, I wished in vain for a little wagon so that I could play "bus" with it. Finally the longed-for hour arrived when my grandmother took pity on me and bought me a very beautiful little wagon. With an indescribable happiness, I pulled it home, but was too small to lift it up the steps alone. Then as my father lifted it over his head and ran up the steps, I broke into tears. My father did not understand and rebuked me: "Silly boy, you have just gotten a new wagon, and instead of being happy, you begin to bawl. What is wrong with you?" I answered him, "Someday it's going to break down!"

That was, if you see it that way, my first religious experience. Although I was still small and had no idea of life, there suddenly came over me a knowledge of perishableness. Precisely because I loved my wagon so, the thought that it would not belong to me forever but would, rather, end up someday at the garbage dump caused me to shudder. This knowledge of the perishableness of things has been with me ever since and has affected me deeply in my theological thought. It has kept me from utopian fantasies, which would lead us to believe, for example, that in this ephemeral world a kingdom of eternal peace might evolve.

Later, as a student, I was personally confronted by the problem of mortality. At twenty years of age I became seriously ill, with an internal infection, and could get around only in a wheelchair. I waited for my death. When the doctors released me to go home for the final round of my life, they openly made known to me their helplessness. One of them read to me a medical evaluation of my disease in which the following sentence appeared: "If no medication is found in a few months, he will certainly die a very painful death."

After a while, the same doctor wrote me that they were experimenting with a new medication that might possibly be of help to me. After the futile attempts of the past, he would of course give me no great hopes. If I were ready for one last try, he would be very glad to treat me one time with the new medication. After all my past disappointments, I could not at first decide to do it. Only because of my despairing mother did I let myself be brought once again into the hospital. I was not a Christian at that time; I was more a fatalist, resigned to accept what would be and to bury all the hopes of youth.

On the medicine bottle were the words, "Danger, Poison!" The reason for this was that the medication was not yet on the market, but would be first used experimentally at university clinics. Therefore the doctors decided to use it in small, carefully guarded doses. They were uncertain about the intensity of its effect.

I still remember it exactly. It was the *green* Thursday of the year of 1933, as the noise of the demonstration of the Nazis, who had just come into power, pressed into the stillness of my hospital room. Then the chief doctor said to me: "My dear Thielicke, you must realize, just as we doctors sorrowfully perceive, that this medication also does not help. We do not want to detain you further. You can now be taken home again. If you wish, you can wait until tomorrow morning. At least you will be home again for Easter."

Then when I was alone—very much alone—I looked at the bottle on which the word "Poison!" was written and from which I had been taking only a few drops daily. In an act of despairing decision, I drank the whole bottle and said to myself: Either it will kill you quickly and save you a painful, slow death, or this overdose will work and make you healthy. That was certainly a naïve view of the alternatives, but that was the way I saw my situation at that time.

When I had finished the bottle, my glance fell on the crucifix, which the nuns had hung in my room. (I took it with me later, and it still hangs in my study.) At that time, Christ was still a stranger to me, but I saw in the cross the picture of his suffering as well as his compassion. I experienced him as my brother and companion and spoke with him. To be sure, I could not rise up to the promise, "This day, you will be with me in Paradise." Though it meant much to me that he also was in the crisis of death. Under this cross I came to terms with my life. I know though that I also asked for forgiveness. With a deep peace, I tried to sleep. I thought: Perhaps you will never awaken again; also, perhaps, you will get well. I had now placed this matter in another hand and let myself rely on it.

That was my first meeting with Christ. It was a very modest one: I had not seen his countenance, but rather touched only a little of the hem of his garment. But it was just as it was in the New Testament: He had felt the touch and turned around to me. Although at that time I was hardly aware of it.

When I awakened, I marveled first of all that I was still alive. I felt a strange, not completely definable vitality, even though the paralysis was still there. My confession of what I had done caused great alarm in the clinic. Since no one knew what the outcome might be, I was scolded terribly and made responsible for all the consequences. But that did not bother me a great deal.

On the following day, I took a few difficult steps, supported by my mother. I got along better every day. After four weeks I marched normally out of that place and as a well person went to the university in order to write my doctoral thesis in theology. Even now after four decades I must take this medicine daily, but I have no more trouble at all. I was even able to get a certificate in sports activities.

It is certainly understandable that this miracle, which seemed outwardly to be entirely within the laws of science, signified a dividing line in the history of my faith. In spite of this, I could not speak of a "conversion" that could be dated exactly as to time. It was rather as if the water level in my life gradually rose and transformed the wasteland of nihilism into a fruitful landscape.

This process actually was a very slow one. In spite of this experience, I was still first of all a novice theologian. Although I had concluded my studies, and was already a Doctor of Philosophy, I had never preached. I attached myself to the university only and was a pure scientist. When I was asked at school about my study plans, I answered the teacher, "I want to study theology." To this he said, "Therefore, you want to be a minister." However, I turned that off indignantly and said, "That I want to avoid if at all possible." Later my schoolmates often reminded me of this remark.

But at that time, I felt exactly so about it. In spite of my Christian upbringing, I was not a Christian. I felt closer to the Greek gods, which I knew very well from my classical studies in high school, than to the Father of Jesus Christ. I was deeply moved by the question concerning the meaning of life, chance and necessity, freedom and the responsibility of man. Theoretically, I wanted to investigate these problems thoroughly. For that reason, I could have studied philosophy. However, as an eighteen-year-old, I said to myself, even the theologians have pondered these questions from time immemorial. They ponder these things not from the point of view of a "clever loner" but rather within the framework of their Christian community. They have not wrestled just theoretically with these problems within the confines of their offices, but rather they have struggled with each other. They have run the risk of physical destruction on the funeral pyre, or under the ax of the executioner. In general, that cannot be said of philosophers. It must have been a very serious matter for the theologians, although for me the problems which concerned them at that time—such as in the framework of the doctrine of the Trinity—appeared very subtle. That the thinkers of the church felt so responsible for their truth impressed me. For that reason, I believed that they were partners in harmonious dialogue. I wanted to discover whether their truth might be capable of bearing the weight of a life built upon it.

With my hospital experience behind me and now being already touched seriously by Christian faith, I still remained to a great extent in the field of pure science and avoided the pulpit. I thought that I might preach when I had achieved full clarity in the realm of thought. That was a standpoint which I today hold as absolutely false. For proclamation does not have its origin in theology, but rather exactly the opposite. The preaching of the gospel, which gives us the happiness of faith, is always the first. It is not until God has so moved us that our thought apparatus also switches on, and we ask: What does this all mean? How do the statements of faith concerning the word, history, nature, and man fit together with what science and my reason say to me? It would be terrible if God should have nothing to do with all of that and kept himself only in the "religious province" and be allowed to demand only our pious feelings.

Therefore I had ended up in a blind alley when I thought that I could achieve clarity concerning God outside the field of proclamation relying only on theoretical endeavors. From such blind alleys, one seldom finds his way out alone. For that reason, a higher hand had to reach once again into my life, even as it had happened in my room at the clinic.

Because I belonged to the Confessing Church and attacked the Nazis with youthful recklessness, I was expelled from my teaching positions at the University of Heidelberg. One of my friends said to me that I could have actually avoided this decree. I could have done so while remaining true to my convictions in a way that would not have irritated the Nazis. He expressed it very nicely with reference to the Bible: "God may well have ordered Daniel fearlessly to stir up the lions' den. He did not order him also to pull the hair of these wild beasts nor to pinch them on the tail." Such I had already done time and again.

Even so, I suddenly found myself and my wife sitting in the street without a job. Also my salary for the moment was stopped. In order to earn my keep, I had to find work again. What else should come to mind but a preaching position, for which I had always studied? At first no one wanted to take me because as an "enemy of the state" I would be a burden to the church. Finally, the honorable Bishop Wurm took me into his church and hid me away in a rather remote location on Lake Constance. Since I was forbidden by the secret police to leave this place of my activity, forbidden to speak anywhere on the outside, and was not allowed to publish a printed line, I was able to—and had to—concentrate completely on my congregation. Now I had to preach.

Today I know this happening brought about a decisive turning point in my life. I noticed that the proclaimed word touched men, that it afforded solace in the horrors of war, and that through it confused and oppressed human beings gained a new hold. After all the years of abstract thought, I took great pains to make myself understandable to simple people and especially to win the hearts of youth. I sought for illustrative pictures and parables, concerned myself with plain, natural speech and noticed suddenly that the saying was true: To whom God gives a position, he also gives understanding. Now I learned to comprehend the happiness of standing in the middle of a congregation and speaking every Sunday to the assembled members.

Later, I was transferred to Stuttgart. There I spoke in the middle of the bombing raids to a church of thousands and noticed how much one's own faith is strengthened when one witnesses faith given to a brother or a sister who stands on the same foundations.

Later, God reached once again into the experience of my faith—just two years ago. Up to that time I always stood as the soloist at the pulpit. I suffered from the fact that the people sometimes were concentrating too much on my person. Recently I found a young associate, who willingly wanted to learn from my experiences. Along with him, I have built up a group who together act and proclaim. We set aside ten evenings at the Michaelis Church in Hamburg for a course in faith for adults. We experienced joy in the fact that people poured in, especially young people.

But we did not want to stand merely on words, we also wanted to do an active service for the kingdom of God. So we went into a prison and concerned ourselves with the prisoners, stood by those who were released as they took their first steps of freedom. We gathered together drug addicts and juvenile delinquents and sought to help them in the name of Jesus.

At present we are working on a course in how to write testimonies of faith. Beginning in September, a hundred thousand copies will be sent across our land. It is our purpose that they will also appear in America.

Through this work together I perceive a wonderful fulfilling of my life. I am passing on the torch, so to speak, and am placing it in young hands. We safeguard ourselves from empty activity. No meeting passes without placing our circle under the word of God. Before we can give to others, we must first of all receive. Before we speak out in the world, we must have spent time at the throne of God. We stay busy in composing the testimony letters, discussing theology with one another, and often there is heated discussion. We do not remain in theoretical corners; rather, we let the process of our thought go on to the hearing. We eat and drink together. Our fellowship is cheerful and casual. There is no deeper happiness than being able to have faith and to be bound up with those who stand on the same foundation of life.

K. Owen White

K. Owen White was born in London, but his family moved to British Columbia when he was five years old. He was a Canadian until he attended the Bible Institute of Los Angeles. He holds his B.A. degree from the University of Louisville, and Th.B., Th.M., and Ph.D. degrees from Southern Baptist Theological Seminary in Louisville.

His first pastorate was the First Baptist Church of Santa Monica, California. He was later pastor of Baptist churches in Gainesville and Atlanta, Georgia, in Washington, D.C., in Little Rock, Arkansas, and of the First Baptist Church in Houston, Texas. He was a member for eleven years, and vice-president for five years, of the Home Mission Board of the Southern Baptist Convention. In addition to service on various committees of the General and State Conventions of the Southern Baptists, he was president of the General Convention in 1963–1964. Before his retirement he was coordinator of Metropolitan missions in Los Angeles.

In addition to numerous articles in denominational publications and study lessons and program materials written for the Sunday School Board of his denomination he has written several books, including *Studies in Hosea, The Book of Jeremiah, Nehemiah Speaks Again.* The pastorate was always the focus of his interest and his first love, and in it he served for over forty years.

It Couldn't Be

K. OWEN WHITE

I CAN GLADLY BEAR TESTIMONY TO THE FACT THAT THE HAND of God has been upon my life in what I consider to be a most unusual way. In order to do this adequately I need to go back to my origin and early life. I was born in London, England. When I was five years old our family decided to move to British Columbia, Canada. There we settled on a ranch about forty-five miles from the nearest town, which was Kamloops. It was real pioneer country: no road on our side of the river, no railroad, no telephones, no schools, no churches, and mail service every two weeks.

In due time (within seven years, actually) the road, the railroad, and the telephone became realities for us. A small log building served as a one-room schoolhouse and also provided a meeting place where we had occasional religious services at which my father sometimes preached as a layman. In England he had been a practicing physician.

Ours was a Christian home where we usually had Bible-reading and prayer around the table after breakfast. My personal feeling as a lad was that some of my father's prayers were unnecessarily long! However, I am deeply grateful for this early background. I never forgot it. My parents were strongly conservative in theology and had an abiding reverence and respect for the Bible as the Word of God. They imparted this deep conviction to me.

When I was about nine years old a fine layman who was temporarily living with us explained to me how to become a

166

Christian and I made a profession of faith. However, I have never been quite sure I fully understood it.

After seven years in this backwoods area, living in a log house, we moved to another community which was slightly more thickly settled and was only twenty-two miles from another small town. This community also had a one-room school where I finished grade school. Being far from town and in very poor economic circumstances, I was unable to attend high school, so at fourteen I went to work on a large farm owned by an English company and began to contribute to the income of the family.

The only religious activity we had was a Sunday-morning service in the schoolhouse. It was sponsored by a Plymouth Brethren family. The services consisted of singing without an instrument from an old hymnbook known as *Hymns for the Little Flock*. Most of the hymns had six to nine stanzas. We started out singing off key and got worse as we proceeded! The message or messages were usually rambling comments by men who came totally unprepared to speak and waited for the Spirit to move them. Not much challenge or inspiration for a lad! The usual attendance was ten or twelve.

However, I can say that my absolute faith in God as a divine person, in Christ as the only Savior, in the Bible as the dependable Word of God, and in heaven and hell as real places never faltered.

After four years and immediately following World War I we moved to the town of Vernon, which at that time had a population of about twenty-five hundred. After a few months, during which I had several temporary jobs, I went to work in a sash and door factory which manufactured doors, windows, cabinets, shelving, screen doors, and other items. We worked ten hours a day and my salary was one dollar a day!

It was here, when I was past sixteen, that my family first began to attend an organized church and Sunday school. It happened to be a Methodist church.

I am sure it was in the purpose of God that at this point I became personally acquainted with a layman in the church, a railroad man who later became my Sunday school teacher. Although he was considerably older, he took a deep personal interest in me and encouraged me in becoming involved in the activities of a class of young people. In due time I became secretary of the class and he and I spent hours together planning activities, which helped me to overcome my timidity, for I was by nature and background bashful and backward.

All this time I was working with a group of godless, profane men who were much older than I. Their influence upon me was not good!

One Sunday evening the service at the church was to be led by the choir. My Sunday school teacher, a very conservative, evangelistic person, was also the choir director. All the songs that night had to do with Calvary. An old-fashioned projector threw some scenes on the screen that were all pictures of Jesus: Jesus at the Last Supper, Jesus in the Garden of Gethsemane, Jesus being betrayed, Jesus in the house of the high priest, Jesus in Pilate's presence, Jesus being "set at nought by Herod and his men of war," Jesus bearing his cross, and finally the scene at Calvary.

A terrible conviction of my own sin and my need for Christ swept over me and deepened as the service continued. What finally broke my heart was the singing of a duet of which the theme was, "It was for *me* that Jesus died on the cross of Calvary."

No invitation was given, no opportunity to make public profession of faith, and I walked home alone and went into my room. Falling down on my knees in the darkness, I wept my heart out and asked God to forgive me and save me for Jesus' sake! I look to that night as the time when I was born again!

God continued to lead me along. In my heart I knew that I must bear witness to this experience among the men I worked with. It was rough going for a green country boy, but the Lord helped me in it.

On Mother's Day in 1920, I made my first attempt to bring a message to the congregation, having been challenged to do so by my Sunday school teacher. This, too, was a rough experience, but it proved to be the beginning of other attempts to speak in public.

One evening shortly thereafter while I was sitting in the home of my friend the teacher, he startled me by saying, "Owen, did it ever occur to you that the Lord might be calling you to be a preacher?" My astonished response was, "Who? Me?" He replied, "Yes, you!" I laughed and answered: "No, of course not. I never even thought of it." He simply said, "I think you ought to."

Although I had only a grade-school education, was timid by nature, and felt totally inadequate, I could not shake off this suggestion and I prayed about it. The conviction grew that God had a place of service for me somewhere, perhaps in some little country church or some isolated mission field. But what could I do about preparation?

About this time my teacher confided in me that he felt God was calling him to preach. We thought and talked about where we might go to school and considered Moody Bible Institute.

Again the hand of God revealed itself. An evangelist came to the local Baptist church and we talked with him. He said, "Well, why don't you consider going to the Bible Institute of Los Angeles, right here on the West Coast?"

I talked with my mother about it and she merely said: "I heard Dr. R. A. Torrey years ago and I see he is the dean there. I know he is sound doctrinally."

To shorten the recital, both my teacher and I enrolled at BIOLA and for two years I sat under the teaching of R. A. Torrey. He was one of the great Bible teachers and preachers of his day. His faith in the Bible as the divinely inspired Word of God made a deep impression on me.

A few months of studying the New Testament with an open heart and mind convinced me that the New Testament way was also the Baptist way of life, and I was baptized into the Calvary Baptist Church of Los Angeles. I am convinced that God had his hand in this.

Upon going home to work at my old trade during the first summer, I was talking with my mother and she said, "When

I was a young woman I heard Dr. Torrey in England and always prayed that at least one of my sons would have some personal contact with him." I asked her why she had not told me when I was trying to decide where I would go to school. She replied, "Because I wanted to be sure God was leading you and that you were not merely following my suggestions!"

BIOLA was right at the heart of the evangelical movement and during the years that I was there I had opportunity to hear literally dozens of the greatest Bible preachers and teachers of that particular time. All of this strengthened my faith in the authenticity and integrity of the Bible as the Word of God.

Following graduation from BIOLA, through a series of events in which once again God's hand was evident, I enrolled as a student at Southern Baptist Theological Seminary in Louisville, Kentucky, and in two years earned the degree of Bachelor of Theology, which was available at that time to men who had no college training. It was my privilege to study under such men as E. Y. Mullins, John R. Sampey, A. T. Robertson, Kyle M. Yates, Sr. Once again my faith in the Bible as God's Word was reinforced!

Returning to the West Coast, I was called to the First Baptist Church, Santa Monica, California. During my BIOLA days I had met a young lady from Denver who happened to come from a Presbyterian home but like myself had become a Baptist. We were married and worked together in Santa Monica for nearly four years.

I realized that I needed further training, so at her urgent suggestion and with some assistance from her father we left the Santa Monica church and went to Louisville once again. Enrolling in the Y.M.C.A. night school, the University of Louisville, and Southern Baptist Seminary all at the same time, I was able to meet the formal educational requirements that were lacking. In the span of five years I was able to earn a B.A., Th.M., and Ph.D.

Mrs. White and I have served together, mostly in the pastorate, for forty-seven years. She holds the same conservative

Biblical views that I do and has consistently witnessed to all people everywhere.

The point I want to make is that through the years we have put our faith in the Bible as the Word of God. Over the portals of BIOLA were the words, "Forever, O Lord, Thy word is settled in Heaven." From the earliest days I felt that the injunction, "Preach the Word," was a divine command that must not and could not be forgotten or forsaken. When frustration and pressure beset me I felt that I could say with Jeremiah, "But his word was in mine heart as a burning fire shut up in my bones, and I was weary with forbearing, and I could not stay" (Jer. 20:9). The Bible is the Word of God which lives and abides forever!

Looking back through the years at the wonderful opportunities extended to us, my wife and I can only marvel at the hand of God in our experience.

When I was serving as president of the Southern Baptist Convention I was invited to preach the dedication sermon for a new Southern Baptist church in the Vancouver area in British Columbia. Through the gracious generosity of others I was privileged to fly from Vancouver to Kamloops in a private plane and then drive up the river to our old farm. For the first time in over fifty years I looked upon the familiar mountains and river, and withdrawing a few yards from the others, I said to myself: It simply couldn't be! That towheaded, barefoot, bashful, ignorant country boy—pastor of the great First Baptist Church, Houston, Texas, and president of the Southern Baptist Convention! That's right—humanly speaking it couldn't be, it was a miracle of the grace of God!